a gourmet's BOOK of BEASTS

author of
CENTURIES OF OWLS
IN ART AND THE WRITTEN WORD

a gourmet's BOOK of BEASTS

faith medlin

Paul S. Eriksson, INC., New York

To Mary Salinda, Anne, and Winfield

CONTENTS

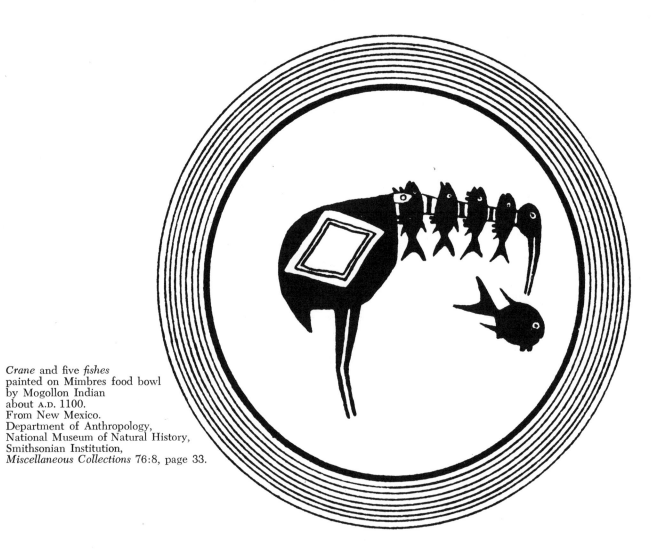

Crane and five fishes
painted on Mimbres food bowl
by Mogollon Indian
about A.D. 1100.
From New Mexico.
Department of Anthropology,
National Museum of Natural History,
Smithsonian Institution,
Miscellaneous Collections 76:8, page 33.

MEATS AND RECIPES

ANIMAL KINGDOM

*(zoological names arranged in about the same order
as the appearance of their ancestors on earth)*

LIST OF ILLUSTRATIONS

ACKNOWLEDGMENTS

The author and publisher wish to thank the libraries, museums, and private collectors for permitting the reproduction of food vessels, paintings, photographs, and drawings in their collections. Photographs have been supplied by the owners or custodians of the works of art, and their courtesy is gratefully acknowledged.

American Museum of Natural History, New York, 37
Art Institute of Chicago, 47, 49, 107
Bettmann Archive, New York, 67
British Museum, London, 7, 19, 25, 53, 58, 96, 129, 153
Brooklyn Museum, New York, 99, 100–104, 114
Buccellati, New York, 11
Buffalo Museum of Science, 29
Campbell Museum, Camden, 162
Cleveland Museum of Art, 4
Lowell Collins Gallery, Houston, 79
County Museum, Truro, England, 124
Denver Art Museum, 40, 83, 135
Detroit Institute of Arts, 60
Duke University Museum of Art, Durham, 170
Field Museum of Natural History, Chicago, 16, 166, 167
Frobenius-Institut, Frankfurt am Main, Germany, 119
Abraham Guillén M., Lima, Peru, 22
Haags Gemeentemuseum, The Hague, 126, 142
Metropolitan Museum of Art, New York, 8, 9, 24, 68, 75, 89, 147, 173
C. P. Meulendijk, Rotterdam, Netherlands, 64
Charles Miles, Oakland, 34
Minneapolis Institute of Arts, 55
Musée Chateau de Blois, Loir-et-Cher, France, 95
Musée de Cluny, Musées Nationaux, Paris, 71
Musée Royal de l'Afrique Centrale, Tervuren, Belgium, 46
Museum of the American Indian, Heye Foundation, New York, 92, 133
Museum of Fine Arts, Boston, 146
Museum voor Land- en Volkenkunde, Rotterdam, Netherlands, 44
Náprstek Museum, Prague, Czechoslovakia, 50
National Museum of Victoria, Melbourne, Australia, 81
Nelson Gallery, Atkins Museum, Kansas City, Missouri, 79
Peabody Museum, Harvard University, Cambridge, 33, 42, 85
Philadelphia Museum of Art, 13
San Antonio Museum Association, Witte Memorial Museum, 63
Smithsonian Institution, Freer Gallery of Art, Washington, D.C., 116
Smithsonian Institution, National Museum of Natural History,
    Department of Anthropology, Washington, D.C., vi, 2, 131, 132, 137, 149
Soprintendenza alle Antichita, Florence, Italy, 27, 150
Steuben Glass, New York, 144
University Museum, Philadelphia, 32, 91, 109
Domingo Seminario Urrutia, Lima-Piura, Peru, 35
Victoria & Albert Museum, London, 87
Wadsworth Atheneum, Hartford, 111, 139
Martin von Wagner Museum der Universität, Würzburg, Germany, 122
Yale University Art Gallery, New Haven, 45

"Preparing for the holiday banquets in a Washington market on the arrival of game meats from the West." From George A. H. Sala's *America Revisited* (London, 1882).

PREFACE

A CAN OF KANGAROO TAIL SOUP was given to us by a neighbor a few years ago, and a week later a Michigan friend sent a tin of baby octopus. Never having eaten these foods, we opened the gifts with awe—and to our relief found them delectable! Cued, thereby, to notice gourmet shelves in the shops, I gradually began to bring home other beasts that might widen the eyes of my young sons or stimulate the palate of my well-traveled husband. As part of some art studies, I also decided to assemble the labels of this curious assortment in a collage on a large serving tray. My zoo grew fantastically.

Why were these foods for sale, I wondered. Because they really did taste good? Because they raised eyebrows, or were expensive or rare? Why eat grasshoppers? Who relishes elephants and tigers? Snakes? Sensational! In time, because of limitations of certain labels from the stores, I started designing my own labels for the tray, and more questions arose. For instance, of all the sharks in the oceans, which kind could properly appear on a shark's fin soup label? What, precisely, did a mouflon look like? Could any old nest be made into bird's nest soup? Since a proper label lists the contents of its can, what ingredients should be printed for Scottish haggis? These puzzles, and many more, led to an intriguing study of cookbooks and animal histories in a great many libraries.

Thoughtful recipes, I found, had been published for almost any animal I cared to trace. A surprising number of unusual fresh or frozen meats proved available, although usually at very high prices.

bear	dove	kangaroo	quail
beaver	eel	moose	raccoon
bison	elk	mussel	reindeer
boar	frog	octopus	snail
conch	goat	opossum	turtle
deer	guinea fowl	pheasant	whale

Abalone and shark's fin could be purchased in dried form. Fresh aardvark, camel, and zebra were not in the markets, but frozen lion, hippopotamus, and rattlesnake were advertised in a game catalog in 1969. Armadillo, blackbird, iguana, porcupine, pronghorn, puma, and squirrel required a willing and perhaps a licensed hunter in a particular part of our country. Every one of these "strange" meats, I came to understand, tasted very good indeed if properly prepared, even though it might be rejected by certain groups of people because of religion, custom, geography, or ecology.

A tray of labels became too small to contain the huge story of animals as food for man, and A GOURMET'S BOOK OF BEASTS grew in its place.

One of the earliest animal histories was written by the Greek philosopher Aristotle about 335 B.C. Most of his work was based on his own observation rather than hearsay, and he laid a solid foundation for the studies in zoology that followed. About A.D. 70 the Roman scholar Pliny the Elder compiled a natural history that codified his own beliefs as well as the opinions of others on the characteristics of animals. Pliny's pronouncements were not always supported by scientific studies, but they were quoted as gospel through most of the Dark Ages.

About A.D. 200 another set of animal writings appeared and became very popular with the common people of Europe and the Near East, although more for its spiritual lessons than for its meager scientific instruction. Called the *Physiologus*, this collection of forty or so animal sermons is generally considered the creation of a monk known as Physiologus, or "the Naturalist," who lived in Alexandria. He described each animal, or perhaps just a portion of that animal, according to the conventional wisdoms of the ancient world and ended each account with a moral, warning the reader not to act like that animal lest he suffer the same ill fate that befell it. Neither the writer nor the reader seemed to care if the description was fanciful, so it often was, as in the case of the hydrus, the griffin, or the ant-lion. The important thing was that the creature have some characteristic that exemplified Good or Evil and could therefore serve the mystical interpretations of religion. Each new manuscript of these nature stories was copied by hand and was often ingeniously edited by the scribe to fit his own notions of the animal's appearance or to serve his own beliefs in God and the Devil. The *Physiologus* usually began with a four-legged lion, followed in no particular order by creatures which included three-legged birds or thousand-legged bugs or no-legged serpents.

During the twelfth to the fourteenth centuries an expanded text known as the *Bestiary*, or *Book of Beasts*, became popular in England. It described and illustrated as many as four hundred animals and again interpreted their behavior according to theological doctrines. Humor and social commentary occasionally slipped into some of the later editions.

With the new insights of life that came with the Renaissance, the beast tales fell out of favor and solid science took over. A great advance was made in 1758 when the animal kingdom was effectively organized according to physiological structure by the Swedish biologist Karl von Linné, also known as Carolus Linnaeus. His binomial system of zoological classification, used throughout the world today, gives each animal two Latin names, the first indicating its genus and the second indicating its species. With additions and revisions by later investigators, over a million species are now described under this system, and they are arranged as much as possible according to the order of the appearance of their ancestors on this earth.

A GOURMET'S BOOK OF BEASTS continues the age-old business of describing animals according to their antics and exteriors, but it also describes the characteristics of each animal's flesh as food for man, and each account ends —not with a moral—but with a recipe for preparation of the meat. Most of the recipes have been developed and tested in my own kitchen; a few quote interesting recipes or experiences of other writers. A bibliography documents each animal with recipe-titles from outstanding culinary authorities. Some of these meats are scarce today, so preliminary recipes were sometimes practiced on standard cuts of beef or chicken or pork and when seemingly perfected were then used on the exotic meat for which the recipe was actually designed. Chicken thus substituted for iguana; beef for sea turtle, whale, elk, moose, reindeer, or bison; domestic rabbit for squirrel; lamb for young camel; ox tail for kangaroo tail; and so forth—so that really many of these recipes are interchangeable and need not be neglected because the specific meat cannot be obtained. Indeed. some animals such as whale and alligator are endangered species whose meat is not now sold in this country.

Almost every animal is illustrated by a food vessel either in the form of that animal or decorated with its picture. A few are depicted in hunting or banquet scenes. All are from outstanding museums and art collections, reflecting the universal interest of the artist and curator as well as the cook in the many beasts that enliven our world today.

A few cookbooks give the Latin name of each animal along with its common English title. This double-naming used to seem mysteriously remote to me before I began to understand the idea of zoological classification. With the hope of bringing the scientific system of nomenclature into sharper focus in the kitchen, the animals in A GOURMET'S BOOK OF BEASTS are not only identified with both their Latin and English names, they are also arranged from the simplest to the most complex as their evolution is thought to have developed. This order is accepted by most, but not all, zoologists today. Biological knowledge is still crystallizing. Specialists who have spent many professional years studying these subjects sometimes come to conclusions that differ from those of their colleagues, and an omnipotent judgment on diverging opinions is a challenge, to say the very least. It is hoped the facts distilled in this book are the best choices of all those available and is also hoped these animal biographies will spare the interested kitchen reader a small measure of searching for information in scattered references far beyond the pantry shelf.

Broadly speaking, a beast is *any living creature*. In more specific circles a beast is *any four-footed animal* as opposed to birds, reptiles, fishes, and insects. In the culinary world a beast is usually understood to be *a quadruped that serves as man's food;* this can include large barnyard animals such as cows and goats, small barnyard animals such as suckling pigs and rabbits, working animals such as elephants or camels, and ground game such as deer and boar. With beastly license, however, this book also includes dwellers of the sea as well as wingéd beings of the sky.

In recent years my food-hunting has been confined to early-morning food-stalls in a Mediterranean village or to supermarkets in New England or Texas, but my supplies haven't always come from a store. I once sailed in a forty-six-foot schooner for fifty-one days without making port; the huge sea turtle we captured a few hundred miles offshore was joyous fare for a crew living without an ice chest. I have also dived for conch in the Bahamas, searched for langosta in the shoals of the Galapagos, stalked wild goats in the Marquesas, and welcomed home the marksman in Alaska. More recently I have come to realize that many of the wild foods we once took for granted are now tottering between reality and oblivion. Expanding human populations take their toll as cement roads pave the forests and contaminants clog the estuaries, and the conservationist becomes increasingly vital to wildlife's survival. Game meats are still available, however. The hunter is at times more helpful than harmful to the balance of nature, and even in special game reservations certain species must occasionally be culled to limit animal populations to available natural foods and stamping grounds. But who knows? Our grandchildren's grandchildren may have to exist on synthetic food tablets, and meat as we enjoy it today may become as fabulous to our descendants as steaks from the prehistoric Mastodon (*Mastodon americanus*) or two-gallon eggs from the extinct, half-ton Elephant Bird (*Aepyornis maximus*) now are to us.

ABALONE

IN THE BEGINNING the animal had one cell. It divided and multiplied and lived in peace within the cosmos. In time, certain of these organisms kept more than one cell to themselves and took on ways unlike their neighbors as they competed for survival. Finally with the passing of many eons some animals could swim only in the surging seas while others crawled upon the shores or leaped the mountain shelves or glided skyward in the wind. Large animals fed upon small animals or on those with lesser guile, and existence was a challenge to them all. When man eventually rose upon the earth, he gathered fruits and nuts and grains to eat, and like the four-footed beasts of the land or the birds of the air or the fishes of the sea before him, he also turned to animals to sustain him in his needs. Among the simplest that he chose were the soft-bodied mollusks of the oceans.

The abalone, like its relatives the conch and snail, has one single spiral shell which is open on the bottom and protects a large muscular foot. This foot is about the same diameter as the shell and is used to creep about and cling tenaciously to coastal rocks. It is this beautifully-housed "steak," so difficult to pry from its anchorage, that is coveted by a hungry man—indeed, by an epicure! Water exits from the animal's gills through the holes near the edge of the shell. Indians used to plug these breathing holes with asphalt so the shell could be used as a food utensil. The iridescent mother-of-pearl shell has been prized by artists of many cultures for making jewelry and inlaid decorations.

In six years the Red Abalone (*Haliotis rufescens*) attains a diameter of 4 inches. In another six years it may measure 7 inches and be of legal size for divers in California. Rarely these days is an abalone left undisturbed to achieve its full potential of 12 inches. The dark outer shell may be camou- flaged by hydroids and other marine hitchhikers as the algae-feeding abalone inches along rocky ledges under ribbons of kelp. The inner facing of the shell reflects the myriad of lustrous colors so enjoyed by the shell collector. An early historical account says the shell of *H. rufescens* was once so valuable an item of trade that a single specimen could be exchanged for one horse.

This surf-loving gastropod once flourished in great numbers between the tides of California shores, but its shell as well as its distinctive meat have been hunted by so many sportsmen and commercial fishermen in recent decades that the oval gem is now scarce, even in deeper waters, and must be rigorously protected by law. California abalone may not be canned, dried, or shipped out of the state. Residents are strictly regulated as to the size of shell, number per day, and time of year they may harvest this slow- growing seafood. Laws protecting smaller species of abalone are very similar in Oregon, Washington, and Alaska. Frozen, canned, or dried

1

Abalone shell from an ancient Indian mound in California, believed buried to serve as a dish in the afterworld the same as it served in life. Length 5½ inches. Department of Anthropology, National Museum of Natural History, Smithsonian Institution, *Bureau of American Ethnology Second Annual Report,* 1880–81, plate XXI.

abalone sold in markets in other states is probably imported from such areas as New Zealand (where it is called *paua*), Japan, or Mexico.

Abalone meat is most flavorful and plump when shucked immediately, although it can be kept alive for a few days in a cool place if covered with a sea-soaked sack. Once expired, it deteriorates quickly. To clean the animal, a knife or wedge is rotated between the soft body and the shell to sever the attaching stalk. The green stomach is discarded. The dark ruffle edging the foot is trimmed away for use in chowder or fritters. The remaining white meat is sliced across the grain into discs about three-eighths-inch thick which then are pounded with a meat hammer or a wooden mallet until tender but not mushy. The flavor of the meat can be improved if the steaks are aged in the refrigerator for a day before cooking. The Japanese score the steak, slice it as thinly as possible, dip the slices in soy sauce, and eat the rich, crunchy delicacy—without cooking—as *sashimi.*

ABALONE WITH GREEN BEANS

½ pound fresh abalone meat

Slice each abalone into discs, tenderize by pounding, and then cut into strips about ¼ inch wide and up to 1½ inches long.

2 tablespoons cornstarch

2 tablespoons Kikkoman soy sauce

2 tablespoons sweet vermouth

Combine cornstarch, soy sauce, and vermouth. Mix thoroughly with abalone strips.

1 pound fresh young green stringbeans (about 4 cups)

½ cup chicken stock

½ teaspoon salt

Remove endtips and strings from each bean, and slice each bean lengthwise into 2 long strips. Bring stock and salt to boil in saucepan. Add beans, cover, and simmer about 8 to 10 minutes—or until beans begin to be tender but are still somewhat crisp.

1 tablespoon vegetable oil

Heat oil in thick-bottomed skillet. Over high heat, sauté abalone for ½ minute, stirring constantly with spatula. Add hot beans and stock. Reduce heat and stir constantly until all ingredients are thoroughly combined. Do not overcook, thereby toughening abalone and fading beans. Serve immediately with white rice* and red crabapples preserved in spices. Serves 4.

(*To prepare rice*: Rinse 1 cup long-grain white rice in plentiful amounts of cold water until starchy appearance of water dissipates. In wide, thick-bottomed pan, bring to boil 2 cups water, 1 tablespoon butter, and ½ teaspoon salt. Scatter rice into water. Stir, cover—leaving a small crack for about 5 minutes and then covering tightly, and simmer for 20 minutes or until moisture is absorbed.)

Colima earthenware vessel
in the shape of a *conch* shell.
From western Mexico,
fifth century (?) A.D.
Height 5⅝ inches,
width 8¾ inches,
length 10 inches.
Courtesy of The Cleveland Museum of Art,
gift of J. H. Wade III, #66.127.

CONCH

HOLD THE SHELL of a queen conch to your ear, and you'll hear the siren song of the sea. Break off the tip of a shell and blow, and you'll sound the bugle-call to dinner. Eat of the succulent flesh of a conch, and 'tis said you'll be young forever. Perhaps Ponce de Leon who left the shores of Spain in fruitless search of the Fountain of Youth passed up this miracle-maker in the New World without recognizing its true worth.

The conch lolls on sandy bottoms of warm, shallow waters in many parts of the world. One of the largest of these algae-feeding sea snails is the Queen Conch (*Strombus gigas*) of the blue Caribbean. It measures as much as 12 inches in length and weighs up to 6 pounds. Most of its white spiral shell is coated with a layer of brownish-yellow horn. The entrance lip, however, radiates inviting shades of pink and orange. The animal's long, narrow foot moving in and out of this enticing doorway has a strong claw for pulling its housetrailer from shoal to shoal. Sometimes the mantle yields a pink pearl.

In readying this mollusk for the kitchen, freezing and then partially thawing the animal makes it easier to remove the meaty body from the shell. Light boiling also helps in tugging the prize from its package. Or generous amounts of salt poured onto a conch's doorway will cause its foot to loosen so the meat can be drawn out. The sweet, rich white meat can be served raw in cocktails and salads, or it can be sliced or ground for fritters, spaghetti sauces, curries, or the celebrated chowders. Frozen or canned meat is available in many city markets, sometimes under the Italian name *scungilli*.

4

CONCH CHOWDER

Meat from 8 fresh conchs

Juice from 2 small limes

Cut meat into ¼-inch slices. Pound slices with meat mallet. Cut slices into ½-inch squares. Marinate in lime juice for about 30 minutes.

¼ cup diced salt pork

1 large Bermuda onion, diced

1 large fresh
sweet green pepper, diced

In large, enamel-coated, thick-bottomed kettle, over low heat, fry pork until brown and crisp. Add onion and green pepper, and sauté for about 2 minutes, stirring frequently. Add conch, and sauté for about 2 minutes.

1 cup clam juice

1 large fresh tomato,
skinned and diced

1 large raw potato, diced

1 tablespoon sugar

½ teaspoon salt

⅛ teaspoon white pepper

⅛ teaspoon thyme

1 small bay leaf

Add clam juice, tomato, potato, sugar, salt, white pepper, thyme, and bay leaf. Cover and simmer until conch and potatoes are tender. Do not overcook. Discard bay leaf.

2 tablespoons flour

2 tablespoons butter

Milk from 1 coconut*

Knead flour into butter. Add to broth, and stir until smoothly thickened. Add coconut milk; heat to serving temperature but do not boil (and thereby risk curdling the liquid). Serve hot, with crisp pilot crackers. Serves 4 to 6.

(*To make coconut milk: With ice pick, pierce the three soft eyes in shell of husked, fresh coconut. Drain coconut water; reserve. Bake shell in preheated 350°F oven for 15 minutes to shrink meat. Pry meat from shell. To coconut water add as much plain water as necessary to obtain ratio of 1 cup liquid to 1 cup coconut meat. If using electric blender: Bring liquid to boil. Combine with small chunks of coconut meat in blender, and chop finely. Set aside for 20 minutes, then pour contents from blender through double layer of cheesecloth into bowl. Press as much liquid as possible from meat through cheesecloth to obtain coconut milk. If using hand grater: Loosely tie grated coconut in double layer of cheesecloth. Place packet in bowl. Pour boiling liquid over packet and let stand 20 minutes before expressing coconut milk.)

5

SNAIL

THE UBIQUITOUS snail thrives in the arctic as well as the tropics and in forests as well as fresh-water ponds and salty seas. Not all species of this adaptable mollusk are suitable for human consumption, however.

A marine snail that is edible is the Common Periwinkle (*Littorina littorea*). It once existed only on the surf-pounded rocks of the eastern coasts of the North Atlantic. About 1850, however, it appeared in the Nova Scotia tidelands and now abounds southward as far as New Jersey. Its striped shell blends from dark olive to black in color. The Lined Periwinkle (*L. irrorata*) which once flourished mainly in the salt marshes edging the Gulf of Mexico has now expanded northward to Cape Cod; its amber shell is dotted with small brown spots. Each of these univalves measures about an inch from its flat, meaty foot to the peak of its 7- or 8-whorled shell. It feeds on algae and seaweeds.

"Winkles" have been popular in England for centuries. Time was when roasted winkles could be bought from hawkers roaming London streets, or boiled winkles could be ordered at tables in special winkle shops. Today, however, fresh periwinkles must usually be purchased by the scoop or bushel at fish markets and then prepared at home. A special stiletto called a winkle pin is used to remove the cooked meat from the shell.

In ancient Rome artful tradesmen catered to the luxury-loving sybarites by cultivating plump land snails. The snails were confined in pens and fattened on honey-like sapa and wheat meal. Today in France the 5- to 7-whorled Edible Snail (*Helix pomatia*) measuring about 1½ inches in diameter is raised on grape leaves, vegetables, and bran mash, and more than 200 million snails are consumed annually in that country alone. Certain edible snails from the tropics measure 6 inches in diameter and weigh a pound apiece.

A snail requires a moist or wet environment. Lacking same, it withdraws into its shell and bolts the door, called an operculum, until times are better. This retirement may last a few days or several years. Unlike the winter hibernation of many animals, a snail's retirement, called estivation, can take place at any season.

Snails taken from free areas rather than from professional snaileries should be deprived of food for three or four days before being prepared for the table. Then the procedure can be as follows: Scrub shells thoroughly. Place them in a large kettle with cold, lightly-salted water. Cover with weighted lid. Soak for half an hour, then change water and repeat the soaking. Drain. Discard shells whose heads are not showing. Pour enough boiling water over snails to cover. Add salt, peppercorns, and bay leaf. Bring to boil, then reduce to simmer. As soon as a head extends, remove meat from shell with nutpick or tweezer. Also remove head and black tip of tail from each snail. Place meat in a small saucepan, add ½ cup white wine plus enough water to cover. Simmer with *bouquet garni* until tender.

The recipe below, while essentially a classic preparation of snail meat, does not require the traditional complicated equipment which might be enough to discourage a cook venturing into snaildom for the first time. The recipe eliminates the conventional use of one snail shell to hold each piece of snail meat, an indented snail platter on which to balance each set of shells, and snail tongs and fork with which to remove each baked tidbit from its shell.

Mochica pottery stirrup vase with representations of *snail* monsters painted and in low relief. From Peru, A.D. 1–900. Trustees of the British Museum, London, #1909.12–18.193.

SNAILS, BREADED

24 giant snails, canned or prepared as above

8 large clam shells or scallop shells or individual baking dishes

4 tablespoons melted butter

Drain the snails. Lightly brush the inside of each serving dish with a bit of melted butter. Place 3 snails on each serving dish. Cut each snail into 3 sections.

2 teaspoons minced shallots

2 teaspoons minced garlic

2 tablespoons fresh parsley, chopped

¼ teaspoon salt

⅛ teaspoon white pepper

4 tablespoons very dry, finely-crushed bread crumbs

In mortar, combine shallots, garlic, parsley, salt, and pepper. Crush and mix with pestle. Add crumbs and remaining butter. Mix thoroughly. Pack mixture flat in the mortar; cut into 8 even wedges. Distribute one wedge over each bed of snail meat. Place filled shells on baking sheet under broiler for 4 minutes or until browned. Serve piping hot. Makes 8 small servings.

7

Silver spoon with bowl in the form of a *scallop*.
Made by Antonio Gentili da Faenza, in Rome, about 1580.
Length 6¾ inches.
The Metropolitan Museum of Art, New York;
Rogers Fund, #47.52.3.

SCALLOP

UNLIKE ITS CLOSE RELATIVES the mussel, oyster, or clam which all reside placidly on sand or rock, the lively scallop is a rapid swimmer that rarely attaches itself to one place. A scallop can zig-zag forward by drawing water inward through the radiating grooves of its two valves (shells) and then forcing streams outward in alternating jets from ears on either side of its straight hinge. Or when fleeing from a starfish or an octopus, it can speed backward by opening and closing its valves rapidly to shoot water out the fan-shaped grooves of its shells. As the scallop thus retreats, it steers blindly with its hinge in the lead, even though fifty eyes with good vision edge the fringe just inside the rim of its trailing shells. Each tiny turquoise eye has a cornea, lens, and optic nerve.

The large adductor muscle that powers the scallop's flapping shells is also sometimes called an eye, and it is this pinkish or cream-colored meat that goes to American markets. Fishermen in the United States customarily separate the muscle from the rest of the body and shell while their boats are still at sea, packing the dressed meat on ice or freezing it on the spot for trans-shipment. In Europe, South America, and the West Indies, fishbuyers obtain the entire body of the scallop so consumers can eat the complete scallop as they would an oyster or a clam, since every bit of the scallop is edible. The shells make useful bowls or baking dishes.

Scallops are found throughout the world in many colors and sizes. The shelter-loving Bay Scallop (*Pecten irradians*) is dredged from shallow waters from Cape Hatteras to Cape Cod; its sharply-ribbed shell grows to a width of 4 inches with an adductor muscle about ½ inch across. The giant Sea Scallop (*P. magellanicus*) is dragged from offshore banks or deep waters from the Carolinas northward; its shell measures up to 8 inches in diameter with a muscle 2 inches across.

SCALLOPS WITH FIDDLEHEADS

2½ cups (10 ounces) fresh or frozen fern fiddleheads

½ cup water

2 tablespoons distilled white vinegar

1 teaspoon white sugar

½ teaspoon salt

Combine water, vinegar, sugar, and salt in stainless steel or enameled saucepan and bring to boil. Drop fiddleheads into boiling liquid. Reduce heat, cover, and simmer for about 5 minutes. Drain and chill.

1½ pounds fresh scallops

3 tablespoons flour

½ teaspoon salt

⅛ teaspoon ground white pepper

3 tablespoons butter

3 tablespoons dry vermouth

Paprika

If scallops are the large variety, cut into ¼-inch slices. Dry thoroughly. Combine flour, salt, and pepper in plastic or paper bag. Toss scallops in bag until thoroughly coated. Melt butter in large skillet. Over medium heat, sauté scallops for about 5 minutes, stirring constantly. Add vermouth, reduce heat, and simmer 5 more minutes, stirring gently. Divide onto 3 plates and sprinkle each serving with paprika. Serve with chilled fiddleheads. Serves 3.

Wedgwood pink lustre dish in the form of a *scallop*.
From England, eighteenth century.
Depth 1⅜ inches, diameter 8 inches.
The Metropolitan Museum of Art, New York; Rogers Fund, #16.17.

MUSSEL

MANY AMERICANS PASS UP A GOOD THING when they veto the mussel as a food. This mollusk which is cultivated as a luxurious delicacy in Europe and yet is all too often neglected as a dining pleasure in this country is one of the most plentiful seafoods available on our coasts. It is easier to gather than other shellfish and because of its paper-thin housing provides more meat per basketful than the thicker-shelled clam or oyster. The meat of a mussel is very tender and has a flavor equal to that of the smallest clam. When steamed, the rich golden color of the eastern mussel and the bright orange hue of some of the western species give pleasant accents to the appearance of dishes at the table.

A mussel has two hinged valves, or half-shells, that fold together to form an ovaloid or crescent-like case. The animal within sustains itself with plants and animals that it siphons and strains from the seawater. The shell of the Blue Mussel (*Mytilus edulis*) of the Atlantic coasts has a blue-black exterior and a pearly-blue or violet interior; it grows to a length of 3 inches or more. The same-sized Brown Mussel (*M. californianus*) of the West Coast which often has orange meat should be eaten only from November through April.

Mussels are highly perishable, and therefore only live ones should be cooked for eating. A shell should be discarded if it lacks a byssus (a beard or tuft of filaments by which the mussel anchors itself to a rock or piling). A mussel should likewise be rejected if its shell does not open in the steaming pot; one that fails to release its latch is probably dead and filled with mud. In many areas mussels should not be harvested and eaten during warm weather when they may have fed on plankton that are toxic to man. Quarantine periods vary according to locale. Fresh-water mussels are not edible. One pound of mussel meat is obtained from about 3.8 pounds of mussels in the shell.

Silver dish with *mussels,* fish, and crayfish on cover.
Courtesy of Buccellati, Fifth Avenue, New York.

MUSSEL COCKTAIL WITH BLACK OLIVES AND PURPLE ONIONS

2 pounds fresh mussels in their shells
¼ cup dry white wine
2 sprigs fresh parsley

Remove beard from each mussel. Under running water, scrub each shell with stiff brush. Place mussels, wine, and parsley in wide pan. Cover. Over high heat, boil for 3 minutes or until shells open. Remove each shell from pan as soon as it opens. Remove meat from shells. Chill meat.

6 crisp lettuce leaves

Tear leaves into bite size and line bottoms of individual cocktail bowls.

1 cup black Greek olives cured in oil, pitted
1 cup diced purple onions

Combine mussels, olives, and onions. Distribute on lettuce in bowls.

1 cup sour cream
2 teaspoons anchovy paste
2 tablespoons small capers

Combine sour cream and anchovy paste. Spoon a mound of dressing over each serving of mussels. Sprinkle capers over dressing. Serve with light beer. Robust servings for 6.

11

OYSTER

He who discovers a valuable pearl in his oyster holds not a mollusk for the kitchen, but he who finds a worthless pearl in his oyster has the promise of one of the finest shellfish dinners the sea can provide. Most pearl oysters are found in tropical waters such as the Persian Gulf or the South Pacific. Edible oysters are found in cooler waters, including all the coastlines of the United States. The common Eastern Oyster (*Ostrea virginica*) of our Atlantic and Gulf coasts grows to a length of 6 inches. The Olympia Oyster (*O. lurida*) of the Pacific reaches a length of 3 inches.

Newborn oysters float freely in brackish bays or river inlets until about two weeks old and then attach themselves to rocks, roots, or shells. Once anchored, they remain on their solid-grounded host for the rest of their lives, which in rare cases may be as long as twenty years. The lodging place must be free of shifting sands or choking mud lest the oyster smother and starve, for this stationary creature depends on clear currents to carry tiny plants and animals to its strainer-mouth for sustenance. An oyster grows to its full size in three or four years.

The cement-colored, erratically-shaped house of the oyster is not a wonder of architectural design coveted by collectors of beautiful shells, but it does have commercial value for making roadbeds as well as cement. The left valve on which the oyster rests is larger, thicker, and more concave than the right valve. These hinged shells are opened and closed by one adductor muscle. When an oyster is shucked for eating that muscle, the wide-lipped ends of the shell, opposite the hinge, are broken with a pair of nippers or by striking the lips against a mounted chisel with a wooden hammer. A knife is then inserted in the newly-made hole and cuts across the strong muscle, thus releasing the tightly-closed valves. The entire soft body is edible and highly nutritious.

Oysters are brought up from shallow tidelands in basket-jawed tongs or from deeper waters in dredges. Their flavor may not be at its best during the summer months, and they may even be toxic as human food at this time if they have been feeding on certain hot-weather protozoa. Also, state laws may prohibit harvesting of oysters during summer spawning. This need not deter the oyster enthusiast from year-round indulgence, however, since quick-frozen oysters shucked at prime season are available in many markets at all times. Oyster farmers frequently move their catches to warm, shallow waters for final fattening before dressing the plump meat for consumers.

Silver salt cellar depicting a cherub
leaning on an *oyster* shell.
By Antoine-Sebastien Durand, France, 1757–1758.
Height 10.6 centimeters, length 21.1 centimeters.
Courtesy of Philadelphia Museum of Art, #46–26–1.

OYSTER SUBMARINES

*4 elongated hard rolls
(each about 2 ounces)
made from French sourdough*

Preheat oven to 350°F. Slice each roll three-fourths through, lengthwise, leaving hinge on one side. Scoop out soft inner bread and tear it into small pieces; place pieces on baking sheet in oven to dry while preparing other ingredients.

*¼ pound bacon, diced
(½ cup, firmly packed)*

Fry bacon in skillet until brown and crisp. Set bacon aside.

¼ teaspoon salt

⅛ teaspoon cayenne pepper

On sheet of waxed paper, crumble and crush dried bread pieces. Mix salt and pepper with bread crumbs.

1 pint freshly-shucked oysters

Place hollowed rolls in oven to heat while oysters are frying. Drain oysters. Coat each oyster with crumbs. Over medium heat, stirring frequently, fry oysters in bacon fat until heated through and plump.

*1 medium-sized
fresh sweet green pepper, diced*

Add bacon pieces, green pepper, and any remaining crumbs to oysters in skillet. Heat briefly. Distribute oyster mixture evenly in rolls. Close rolls. Serve hot. Serves 4.

CLAM

THE PURPLE PORTION of the quahog clam shell was often more valuable than gold when colonists from Europe began trading with the Indians of North America. For centuries the coastal Indians had used shells, not coins, for money. From large shells they skillfully ground cylinders, one-fourth inch long and half as wide, and then drilled a hole down the center of each cylinder. When strung on thongs, these polished beads were called wampum. Purple wampum made from clam shells was worth twice as much as white wampum made from whelk shells. According to the official rate in Massachusetts in 1640, four white beads equaled one penny. Beads were sometimes woven into patterns or belts and worn as personal adornment.

The clam, a bivalve mollusk whose name derives from the word "clamp," lives on or just beneath the surface of sandy or muddy shores of both salt and fresh waters. Growth rings arc from the hinge of its two shells, much as water ripples from a stone thrown into a quiet pool. A clam burrows and moves about on a soft foot. It eats and breathes water-borne food and oxygen that are drawn in one siphon and passed out another siphon.

The Round or Hardshell Clam (*Mercenaria mercenaria*), which is common in protected waters of the Atlantic coast from New England southward, grows to a diameter of 6 inches. This clam lives just below the surface of muddy sand. It is raked or dredged from waters up to six fathoms deep or can be brought up from the shallows in the barefooted grasp of a casual beachcomber. The hardshell clam is known by three names: *littleneck*, which is 3 or 4 years old with a diameter of about 1½ inches, or *cherrystone*, which is about 5 years old with a diameter of about 2 inches—either of which can be eaten raw on the halfshell or can be steamed; or *quahog*, with a diameter of 3 or more inches—used for chowders or stuffed clams.

The Longneck, Steamer, or Softshell Clam (*Mya arenaria*) abounds in tidelands from South Carolina northward and from San Francisco northward. Its thin, oval valves that never quite close grow to a length of 4 inches. This clam burrows in the sand and squirts bubbles to the surface from its long neck that contains the two siphons. It is taken by digging.

Sand can be removed from hardshell clams by immersing them for 15 minutes in clean sea water (or ⅓ cup salt per 1 gallon of tap water) to which a handful of cornmeal has been added; this procedure should then be repeated twice more. Softshell clams can be cleansed in either tap or sea water; this water should be changed twice a day for two days, with a handful of cornmeal added to each water bath.

Clams in the shell should be alive at the time kitchen preparations are begun. Hardshell clams that are not firmly shut should be discarded. Softshell clams whose necks do not constrict slightly when touched should not be used.

Black jade dish in the shape of a shell, with three smaller shells
(including two *clams*) carved in high relief on the bottom.
Not visible, on the top of the dish, are two crabs with a lotus stalk.
From China, K'ang-Hi period, 1662–1722.
Courtesy of Field Museum of Natural History, Chicago, #182676.

CLAMS WITH GREEN SAUCE AND SPAGHETTI

4 dozen fresh hardshell clams in their shells (about 5 pounds)

1 cup water

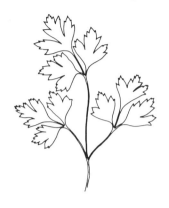

Scrub each clam with stiff brush under running water. Place 1 cup water and half the clams in large kettle over medium heat. As soon as each clam opens, remove it with tongs to a cooling tray. Similarly cook remaining clams in same water. Remove clam meat from each shell and discard shell. Place clam meat in ovenproof bowl with cover; reserve. Strain broth from both the kettle and the cooling tray through several layers of cheesecloth into saucepan; reduce broth to ¾ cup. Reserve broth.

4 quarts boiling water

½ tablespoon salt

1 tablespoon olive oil

8 ounces thin white spaghetti

2 tablespoons melted butter

Add salt and olive oil to water boiling in large kettle. Add unbroken spaghetti, separating with fork. Continue boiling to desired tenderness. Drain. Stir in butter. Place in ovenproof bowl with cover; reserve.

2 slices fresh white bread

¼ cup lemon juice

1 clove garlic, minced

½ teaspoon salt

¼ teaspoon ground black pepper

1 cup firmly-packed fresh Italian parsley (not curly-type parsley)

¼ cup olive oil

½ cup grated Parmesan cheese

Cut off and discard crusts from bread slices. Crumble remainder of slices into electric blender; chop, obtaining about 1 cup moist crumbs. Add ¾ cup clam broth, lemon juice, garlic, salt, pepper, and parsley. Blend until parsley is puréed. With motor on low speed, *very* slowly add olive oil. Then add cheese; blend. Just before serving, reheat spaghetti and clams in covered bowls in preheated 350°F oven until hot enough to serve. Heat green sauce in top of double boiler; serve as soon as hot, to avoid loss of color and to prevent separation of ingredients. Distribute spaghetti on individual plates, dot with clams, and top with sauce. Serves 4.

OCTOPUS

THE HUMANESQUE EYES peering from the tentacled hood of the awesome octopus may seem to justify its reputation as a devil-monster, but in truth this sprawling creature is a shy introvert that prefers to turn its back on man. It has been observed putting its complex brain to more useful purposes than spooking human swimmers by, for example, shrewdly installing a stone in the crack of the shell of a feeding clam, the better to reach in at leisure to dine on the helpless captive.

An octopus, a cuttlefish, and a squid are all cephalopods, meaning animals with feet on their heads. Each foot is actually a ring of eight or ten suction-cupped arms surrounding a head. In the middle of this ring are two horny beaks projecting from a mouth. All cephalopods are carnivorous, feeding principally on crustaceans. All swim by jet propulsion, forcing water through a funnel that thrusts them backwards or forwards. All can eject an ink-like fluid that enables them to elude their enemies through a dark cloud. With varying degrees of success, all can camouflage their bodies by changing their skin colors to match their surroundings.

The Common Octopus (*Octopus vulgaris*) has eight tentacles spreading out from the oval bag that forms its shell-less head, and it extends as much as 10 feet from tip to tip. This muscular creature usually crawls about on its suction cups even though it is capable of jet-propelled swimming if desired. It spends most of its time alone in rocky crevices, emerging only to search for food. There is a Pacific species measuring more than twice the length of *O. vulgaris*, but most octopuses of the world are much smaller.

The Common Cuttlefish (*Sepia officinalis*) of the Mediterranean has an oval body about 6 inches long which is edged with a thin, frilly fin and disguised by variable patterns of spots and stripes. Its spongy, calcified internal shell is called a cuttlebone. Eight of its suckered arms are short; the other two are long tentacles with enlarged outer tips that reach out for prey and also coil into pockets behind the eyes. By day the cuttlefish buries itself in shallow sandy bottoms; by night it hunts in deeper waters.

The American Squid (*Loligo pealeii*) of the Atlantic has a long slender body with two rear fins. It is gray with red spots, subject to camouflaging changes. Like the cuttlefish, two of its ten sucker-bearing arms are longer than the others. Most species of squid measure 8 to 20 inches in length, although there is a giant which stretches to 50 feet. The squid's transparent "shell" is nothing but a soft internal plate, called a pen. Swiftest of all marine invertebrates, this sea-arrow travels in schools near the water's surface. Squids are common throughout the world.

The gastronomic virtues of cephalopods are well recognized by the Italians, Greeks, Chinese, and Japanese who eat the meat in quantity. One hundred grams of the edible portion of raw squid, excluding water, contain 78 calories and 16.4 grams of protein.

Mycenean ceramic jar with *octopus* design.
From Ialysus, Rhodes, 1400–1300 B.C.
Height 40 centimeters.
Trustees of the British Museum, London;
given by John Ruskin.

Most cephalopods must be tenderized by pounding before cooking. C. S. Sonnini described one method of treating an octopus in *Travels in Greece and Turkey* in 1778: "In order to soften the membraneous substance . . . it is beaten for some time or thrown repeatedly, and with force, against the rocks, and at the same time moistened with fresh water." More recent reports from Hawaii tell of islanders pounding their octopuses throughout the night in old washing machines kept for that purpose. If sprinkled with salt, the slippery dark skin of an octopus can be removed readily from the boneless white tentacles which are then easily sliced and pounded with a meat hammer. The chopped meat can be combined with bread stuffing and conveniently baked in the octopus head which is as smooth as a light bulb, inside as well as outside.

SQUID RED SAUCE WITH SEA SHELLS

3 pounds fresh, small squid

Cut off and mince tentacles; reserve. Slit body along stomach from neck to tail. Discard head, ink sac, viscera, and transparent pen. Slip off purplish skin. Rinse remaining white flesh in fresh water. Spread on cutting board and slice into ½-inch squares.

12 fresh scallions

Cut off base roots and most of the green tops. Cut several slits from white base to within ½ inch of green end of each scallion. In large bowl cover scallions with ice cubes and water. Set aside so free ends will flare.

2 tablespoons olive oil
2 large cloves garlic
¼ cup dry red wine

Peel each garlic clove and cut it in half. Over low heat, sauté garlic in oil for 1 minute; mash and discard garlic. Add chopped squid meat, and sauté for 5 minutes, stirring occasionally. Add wine, and simmer for 5 minutes.

1¾ cups (15 ounces)
canned tomato sauce
¾ cup (6 ounces)
canned tomato paste
1 teaspoon dried basil
1 teaspoon dried oregano
½ teaspoon salt
¼ teaspoon ground white pepper
⅛ teaspoon fennel

Add tomato sauce, tomato paste, basil, oregano, salt, pepper, and fennel. Simmer, uncovered, for 45 minutes or until meat is tender and sauce is desired consistency.

6 to 8 quarts boiling water
1 tablespoon salt
1 tablespoon olive oil
1 pound Italian pasta
in form of sea shells
3 tablespoons melted butter
12 tablespoons
grated Parmesan cheese

Add salt and olive oil to water boiling in large kettle. Add pasta shells, stirring occasionally. Cook to desired tenderness. Drain. Gently mix butter with shells. Divide shells onto 6 preheated plates. Ladle hot squid sauce over shells. Sprinkle with grated Parmesan cheese. Garnish with scallion whisks. Serves 6.

SHRIMP

As MANY AS TEN TIMES during the first weeks of its life the tiny shrimp larva sheds its crisp, nearly-clear shell for larger gear as it drifts from deep-sea origins into quiet coastal tide pools or mud flats. Several months later it goes into a final, fast growth spurt, leaves the shorelines of its childhood, and heads for adventure on the high seas. There, if it succeeds in eluding the net of a fisherman or the jaws of a larger fish, this hump-backed crustacean eats its fill of small sea animals and plants. At spawning time in the spring in these same open waters, a female lays as many as a million eggs which sink to the sea bottom, hatch in twenty-four hours, then slowly drift to protected coasts to fulfill another family cycle.

Like its fellow-decapods the lobster and crab, a shrimp has five pairs of jointed legs attached to its head; unlike its large-fisted relatives, however, a shrimp has pincers which are very small. Five pairs of swimmerets are attached to its edible abdomen or tail. Two long antennae signal warnings of danger. One threat to these feelers and whssssh! the shrimp swims swiftly backwards under power of its fanlike tail.

The White Shrimp (*Peneus setiferus*) of the Gulf, measuring up to 6 or 7 inches in length, is the most important commercial species in the United States. The Pacific Shrimp (*Crangon franciscorum*), growing up to 3 inches in length, is heavily fished on the west coast. The True Prawn (*Palaemonetes vulgaris*), up to 9 inches in length, is found in the North Atlantic. Shrimp are fished all year round, but the heaviest catches are made from August to December.

The tail of the shrimp is the only meaty portion of importance as human food. Head and thorax are usually removed on the fishing boat or discarded at the packing plant. Heads-off shrimp are sold according to the number of tails per pound with, for instance, 6 to 8 jumbo prawn tails from India making a pound, or 30 to 60 small shrimp tails from Alaska making a pound. A shrimp may appear grayish-green, coral, or reddish brown when still raw (or "green," according to market terminology). When cooked, however, all shrimps turn pink or red near their translucent casings, and the gray meat within firms to a succulent, delicate white.

Chimú ceramic vessel
in the form of a fisherman with net and *shrimps*.
From Peru, Inca epoch.
Abraham Guillén M., Lima, Peru.

SHRIMPS BROILED SPICILY

¼ cup vegetable oil

1 tablespoon chili powder

2 tablespoons lemon juice

1 teaspoon dried peppermint leaves

1 teaspoon turmeric

½ teaspoon salt

¼ teaspoon ground white pepper

1 clove garlic, bruised

*Fresh jumbo shrimps
or prawns, about 2 pounds
after shelling & deveining*

Combine oil, chili powder, lemon juice, peppermint, turmeric, salt, pepper, and garlic. Marinate shrimps in spice mixture for half an hour, rotating occasionally. Discard garlic. Arrange shrimps in large, shallow baking dish so shrimps do not overlap each other. Place dish about 4 inches under broiler. Broil a few minutes on each side until shrimps are just cooked through; broiling too long will toughen them.

½ cup plum jam

Combine pan drippings and any remaining marinade with jam. Heat and serve in individual bowls as condiment accompanying shrimps. Serve with boiled white rice (recipe on page 3). Serves 4 to 6.

22

LOBSTER

THE GARGANTUAN lobsters, 5 to 6 feet long, that were caught along our northern coast when Europeans began colonizing America have long since disappeared. The usual size to reach the market today is 1 to 2 feet long, weighs from 1 to 3 pounds, and is from 5 to 8 years old. This dark green American Lobster (*Homarus americanus*) of the North Atlantic is distinguished by large pincers on its front pair of legs; the heavier of these claws has blunt teeth for crushing its captive, while the smaller, swifter claw has sharp teeth for tearing food to pieces. This crustacean usually crawls about on ten legs but relies on strokes of its strong fantail to propel it rapidly in an emergency. It prefers to live in burrows or crevices on rocky bottoms though fares well enough on hard sand covered with occasional large seaweeds.

This night-prowler is sometimes frowned upon as a scandalous cannibal. Occasionally it does eat molting or wounded lobsters, dead or alive, but it is fastidious in requiring that the meat—be it lobster, clam, fish, or gull—is not too ripe. A fisherman must periodically freshen a soured bait-holder with scrub brush and sunbath if he expects to lure the coveted lobster to his trap. It is found in depths exceeding 1,200 feet, although 200 feet is the practical limit for most fishermen to work their traps or pots economically.

Throughout most of its life a lobster periodically gets too large for its shell, splits the hard casing down the center of its back, precariously crawls out, and in its vulnerable state hides in rocky crevices until a soft new coat expands and hardens. Unlike the flesh of a soft-shelled crab that is particularly delicious during a similar molting stage, the meat of a molting lobster is stringy and unpalatable. Experienced fishermen recognize the condition of a lobster about to switch its toggery and reject such a specimen for the market.

The 8- to 16-inch West Indian Spiny Lobster (*Panulirus argus*) of warmer Atlantic waters and the West Coast Spiny Lobster (*P. interruptus*) lack large front pincers but wield long antennae to stun their prey. The knobbed brown shells of these species, which are sometimes called sea crayfish or langouste, are often spotted with bright colors.

Whatever the color of a lobster when alive, it turns a bright red when cooked. If straightened out after cooking, its tail will spring back quickly under its body if it was a healthy specimen.

Crayfish are smaller fresh-water relatives of the ocean-dwelling lobsters and are found on every continent except Africa. The Louisiana Crayfish (*Cambarus clarki*) of southern sluggish waters has its counterpart in streams of the Ozarks and Wisconsin as well as in brooks of Pennsylvania and New York.

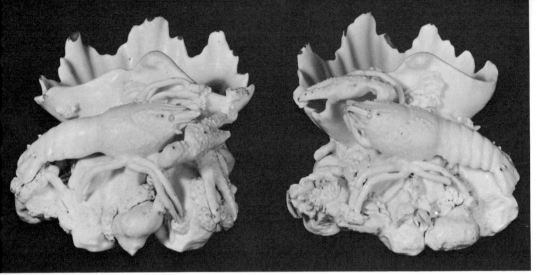

Pair of white porcelain salts,
each in the form of a shell
with moss and coral markings
supported by a *crayfish*.
From Chelsea, England, 1745–1750.
Height 2¾ inches, width 4¼ inches.
The Metropolitan Museum of Art, New York;
collection of Irwin Untermyer.

LOBSTER SALAD WITH ORANGES AND ARTICHOKES

1 package (9 ounces)
frozen artichoke hearts

Two 1½-pound live
North Atlantic lobsters

1 cup dry white wine

Unwrap artichokes for easier handling later. Kill each lobster instantly by inserting sharp knife into crease where tail joins body. Wash lobsters thoroughly. Heat wine to simmering point in large stainless steel or enamel-coated kettle. Add lobsters, cover, and simmer for 20 minutes. Remove and cool lobsters. Strain wine stock into clean pan and bring to boil. Drop in artichokes, cover, and simmer for 10 minutes. Remove and chill artichokes. Remove meat from claws and legs. Discard stomach sac behind head and pull out intestinal vein that runs down the tail. Reserve greenish liver (tomalley) and orange eggs (coral). Remove shell from tail and slice meat.

2 tablespoons fresh (or
2 teaspoons dried) parsley

1 tablespoon Pernod

½ cup mayonnaise

In small bowl, mash liver and eggs. Blend in parsley, Pernod, and mayonnaise. Mince any small shreds of meat and add to sauce.

8 to 12 lettuce leaves

4 navel oranges,
quartered and sliced

Cover 4 salad plates with lettuce. Spoon sauce in line across center of each plate. Arrange meat on top of sauce. Arrange oranges on one side of lobster and artichokes on other side. Serves 4.

CRAB

THE HARD-SHELLED CRAB and the soft-shelled crab are one and the same creature—the Blue Crab (*Callinectes sapidus*) of the Atlantic, the description depending only on how recently the crab shed its hard, tight-fitting coat for a larger covering that is still soft. The boiled or broiled meat of the hard-shelled crab is removed from its casing before serving, while the soft-shelled can be eaten in its entirety, legs and casing included. An average adult crab measures 5 inches across its flattish, oval back and half that distance fore and aft. Its brownish-green carapace has ten teeth, or horns, along the front edge, and its five pairs of blue legs have red-tipped claws. Large front legs have strong pincers to aid the pugnacious crab as it scavenges for carrion or lively beasties along muddy river mouths and brackish bays. Paddle-like rear legs are flat for swimming. A crab usually walks sideways, although it is capable of moving in any direction without bothering to swivel its body. Big and wise is the sidestepper that manages not to walk into a fisherman's wicker trap, or rejects a lineman's hook, or dodges a boatman's spear.

The Dungeness Crab (*Cancer magister*), found from California to the Aleutians, weighs from 1½ to 3½ pounds and measures 6 to 10 inches from horn to horn across its reddish-brown, granular shell.

The Alaska King Crab (*Paralithodes camtschatica*) of North Pacific waters weighs from 6 to 20 pounds and measures as much as 6 feet from leg-tip to leg-tip. Four pairs of legs are visible; a small fifth pair is folded within the gill chamber. The Alaska King Crab is not to be confused with the Horseshoe Crab (*Limulus polyphemus*) of the American Atlantic coast and the Asiatic Pacific coast which is also sometimes called a King Crab but is not used for food in most areas. The Horseshoe Crab, one of the few survivors of a prehistoric group, is related to land spiders and scorpions and is not classified in the order Crustacea.

A crab is very perishable and should be alive at the time it is cooked. About three-and-a-half pounds of whole crab yield a pound of firmly-packed meat. Most of the canned flakes available in stores come from Dungeness crabs.

CRAB ROLLS

½ cup minced scallions

1 tablespoon vegetable oil

1 cup (8 ounces) canned or freshly-cooked crab meat, drained and shredded

½ cup fresh or frozen Chinese snow peas, sliced crosswise into narrow strips

½ cup minced celery

1 tablespoon soy sauce

½ teaspoon monosodium glutamate

Over low heat, sauté scallions in oil for a minute. Add crab meat, snow peas, celery, soy sauce, and monosodium glutamate. Stir gently until warmed through. Strain, or spread onto plate lined with paper towels so juices will be blotted from solid food.

3 large eggs

¾ cup water

¼ cup dry sherry

¾ cup flour

¼ cup cornstarch

½ teaspoon salt

Vegetable oil

Combine eggs, water, and sherry in medium-sized bowl. Beat with wire whisk until blended. Combine flour, cornstarch, and salt. Sift dry mixture into liquid mixture, stirring only until batter is smooth. On stovetop over medium heat, preheat 10-inch skillet and brush inside surface with oil. Using ladle with 3-tablespoon capacity, pour 1 ladleful of batter into skillet. Quickly tilt skillet to spread batter as thinly as possible. Fry on one side until cooked—about a minute. Do not turn over pancake. Transfer pancake to wet tea towel, browned side facing up. Repeat until 12 pancakes are obtained, each time brushing oil on skillet and stirring batter. Distribute 1/12 crab mixture near edge of each pancake. Lap pancake edge over mixture, roll toward center, turn in pancake sides, and roll toward fourth edge to seal. Rolls can be stored in damp towel until final sautéing, arranged so they do not touch each other. Just before serving, sauté rolls in small amount of butter or vegetable oil until browned. Yield: 12 crab rolls.

Ceramic vase
in the form of a *grasshopper*.
From Etruria,
seventh to sixth centuries B.C.
Soprintendenza alle Antichita,
Florence, Italy, #71197.

GRASS HOPPER

THE CLOUDS OF LOCUSTS that used to descend on fields and orchards in this country and devour all the foliage in their pathway were dreaded by many generations of farmers who knew that hard times and even starvation for their families would follow. Exceptions to this fearful group were Indians of the Southwest who long before had learned that locusts themselves were nourishing and even tasty if ground into meal or grilled over hot coals. Today in America entomologists control most of the plagues that fly over farmlands, and roasted grasshoppers are served infrequently as food. Perhaps at a cocktail party a grasshopper hors d'oeuvre is offered as a conversation piece and possibly gains converts on its own crunchy merits when sampled.

As an arthropod (or animal with jointed limbs and with a horny "skeleton" on the outside of its body), the grasshopper is a relative of the shrimp and lobster. As an insect (or animal with its body divided into three parts), it is an even closer relative of the butterfly, bee, and beetle. The grasshopper's *head* has one pair of antennae; each of the three segments of its *thorax* bears a pair of slender legs, with each of the two rear segments usually having a pair of wings; its *abdomen* carries large hearing organs. The male serenades his ladylove with high-pitched noises made by rubbing his front wings against the thick thighs of his hind legs or by rubbing front wings against hind wings as he flies. In the fall the female deposits her eggs, twenty-five to a hundred at a time, in a hole just beneath the surface of the ground. In the spring the eggs hatch into nymphs which mature into grasshoppers in about ninety days. A few weeks after reaching adulthood, the grasshoppers die.

The name grasshopper can be applied to any locust, but the name locust commonly refers only to the migratory, destructive phase in the life of certain grasshoppers with short horns or antennae. A grasshopper can leap twenty times the length of its body. A locust can fly as far as twenty miles in one day. It was the one-inch Rocky Mountain Grasshopper or Locust (*Melanoplus spretus*) that devastated the western plains in 1818–1820, 1855–1857, 1864–1867, and 1874–1878. For centuries the Migratory Locust (*Locusta migratoria*) has periodically appeared in northern Africa.

GRASSHOPPERS RILEY

(Preparation of the grasshopper as a food was explained by the pioneering entomologist Charles Valentine Riley in the proceedings of the American Association for the Advancement of Science in 1875:)

"With the exception of locusts, most other insects that have been used as food for man are obtained in small quantities, and their use is more a matter of curiosity than of interest. They have been employed either by exceptional individuals with perverted tastes, or else as dainty tit-bits to tickle some abnormal and epicurean palate. Not so with locusts, which have, from time immemorial, formed a staple article of diet with many peoples and are used to-day in large quantities in many parts of the globe.

". . . [Locusts] are counted among the 'clean meats' in Leviticus (xi:22), and are referred to in other parts of the Bible, as food for man. . . . Some African tribes have been called *Acridophagi*, from the almost exclusive preference they give to the [locust] diet. We have it from Pliny that locusts were in high esteem among the Parthians, and the records of their use in ancient times, as food, in southern Europe and Asia, are abundant. This use continues in those parts of the world to the present day. . . . Many of our North American Indian tribes, notably the Snake and Digger Indians of California, are known to feed upon [locusts]. . . .

"The records show us that in ancient times these insects were cooked in a variety of ways. *Oedipoda migratoria* and *Acridium perigrinum*, which are the more common devastating locusts of the 'old World,' are both of large size, and they are generally prepared by first detaching the legs and wings. The bodies are then either boiled, roasted, stewed, fried or broiled. The Romans are said to have used them by carefully roasting them to a bright golden yellow. At the present day, in most parts of Africa, and especially in Russia, they are either salted or smoked like red herrings. . . . Some of our Indians collect locusts by lighting fires in the direct path of the devouring swarms. In roasting, the wings and legs crisp up and are separated, the bodies are then eaten fresh or dried in hot ashes and put away for future use. Our Digger Indians roast them, and grind or pound them to a kind of flour, which they mix with pounded acorns, or with different kinds of berries, make into cakes and dry in the sun for future use.

"It had long been a desire with me to test the value of this species (*spretus*) as food, and I did not lose the opportunity to gratify that desire which the recent locust invasion into some of the Mississippi Valley states offered. I knew well enough that the attempt would provoke to ridicule and mirth, or even disgust, the vast majority of our people, unaccustomed to anything of the sort, and associating with the word insect or 'bug,' everything horrid and repulsive. Yet I was governed by weightier reasons than mere curiosity; for many a family in Kansas and Nebraska was last year brought to the brink of the grave by sheer lack of food, while the St. Louis papers reported cases of actual death from starvation in some sections of Missouri, where the insects abounded and ate up every green thing, the past spring.

". . . Commencing the experiments with some misgivings, and fully expecting to have to overcome disagreeable flavor, I was soon most agreeably surprised to find that the insects were quite palatable, in whatever way prepared. The flavor of the raw locust is most strong and disagreeable, but that of the cooked insects is agreeable, and sufficiently mild to be easily neutralized by anything with which they may be mixed, and to admit of easy disguise, according to taste or fancy. But the great point I would make in their favor is, that they need no elaborate preparation or seasoning. They require no disguise, and herein lies

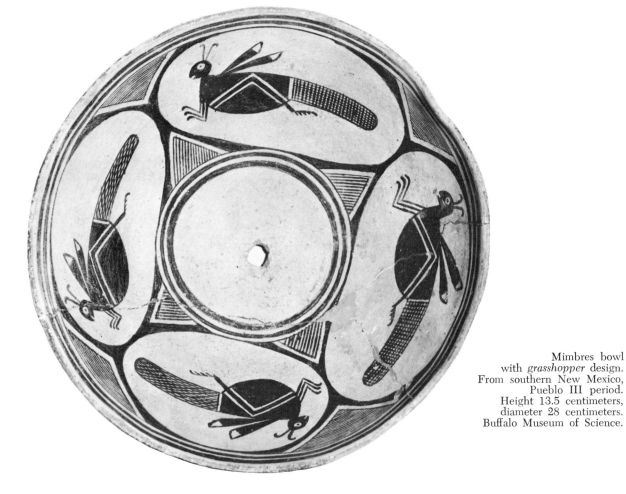

Mimbres bowl
with *grasshopper* design.
From southern New Mexico,
Pueblo III period.
Height 13.5 centimeters,
diameter 28 centimeters.
Buffalo Museum of Science.

their value in exceptional emergencies; for when people are driven to the point of starvation by these ravenous pests, it follows that all other food is either very scarce or unattainable. A broth, made by boiling the unfledged *Calopteni* for two hours in the proper quantity of water, and seasoned with nothing in the world but pepper and salt, is quite palatable, and can scarcely be distinguished from beef broth, though it has a slight flavor peculiar to it and not easily described. The addition of a little butter improves it, and the flavor can, of course, be modified with mint, sage, and other spices, *ad libitum.* Fried or roasted in nothing but their own oil, with the addition of a little salt, and they are by no means unpleasant eating, and have quite a nutty flavor. In fact, it is a flavor, like most peculiar and not unpleasant flavors, that one can soon learn to get fond of. Prepared in this manner, ground and compressed, they would doubtless keep for a long time. Yet their consumption in large quantities in this form would not, I think, prove as wholesome as when made into soup or broth; for I found the chitinous covering and the corneous parts—especially the spines on the tibiae—dry and chippy, and somewhat irritating to the throat. This objection would not apply, with the same force, to the mature individuals, especially of larger species, where the heads, legs and wings are carefully separated before cooking; and, in fact, some of the mature insects prepared in this way, then boiled and afterward stewed with a few vegetables, and a little butter, pepper, salt and vinegar, made an excellent fricassee.

"Lest it be presumed that these opinions result from an unnatural palate, or from mere individual taste, let me add that I took pains to get the opinions of many other persons. Indeed, I shall not soon forget the experience of my first culinary effort in this line—so fraught with fun and so forcibly illustrating the power of example in overcoming prejudice. This attempt was made at an hotel. At first it was impossible to get any assistance from the followers of the *ars coquinaria.* They could not more flatly have refused to touch, taste or handle,

29

had it been a question of cooking vipers. Nor love nor money could induce them to do either, and in this respect the folks of the kitchen were all alike, without distinction of color. There was no other recourse than to turn cook myself, and operations once commenced, the interest and aid of a brother naturalist and two intelligent ladies were soon enlisted. It was most amusing to note how, as the rather savory and pleasant odor went up from the cooking dishes, the expression of horror and disgust gradually vanished from the faces of the curious lookers-on, and how, at last, the head cook—a stout and jolly Negress—took part in the operations; how, when the different dishes were neatly served upon the table and were freely partaken of with evident relish and many expressions of surprise and satisfaction by the ladies and gentlemen interested, this same cook was actually induced to try them and soon grew eloquent in their favor; how, finally, a prominent banker, as also one of the editors of the town joined in the meal. The soup soon vanished and banished silly prejudice; then cakes with batter enough to hold the locusts together disappeared and were pronounced good; then baked locusts with or without condiments; and when the meal was completed with dessert of baked locusts and honey *a la* John the Baptist, the opinion was unanimous that that distinguished prophet no longer deserved our sympathy, and that he had not fared badly on his diet in the wilderness. . . .

"I sent a bushel of the scalded insects to Mr. Jno. Bonnet, one of the oldest and best known caterers of St. Louis. Master of the mysteries of the cuisine, he made a soup which was really delicious and was so pronounced by dozens of prominent St. Louisians who tried it. . . . Mr. Bonnet declared that this locust soup reminded him of nothing so much as crawfish bisque, which is so highly esteemed by connoisseurs. He also declared that he would gladly have it on his bill of fare every day if he could get the insects. His method of preparation was to boil on a brisk fire, having previously seasoned them with salt, pepper and grated nutmeg, the whole being occasionally stirred. When cooked they are pounded in a mortar with bread fried brown, or a puree of rice. They are then replaced in the saucepan and thickened to a broth by placing on a warm part of the stove, but not allowed to boil. For use, the broth is passed through a strainer and a few croutons are added. I have had a small box of fried ones with me for the past two months, and they have been tasted by numerous persons, including the members of the London Entomological Society and of the *Society Entomologique de France*. Without exception they have been pronounced far better than was expected, and those fried in their own oil with a little salt are yet good and fresh; others fried in butter have become slightly rancid—a fault of the butter.

". . . I can safely assert, from my own personal experience, that our Rocky Mountain locust is more palatable when cooked than some animals that we use on our tables. I mention the species more particularly, because the flavor will doubtless differ according to the species, or even according to the nature of the vegetation the insects were nourished on. I have made no chemical analysis of this locust food, but that it is highly nourishing may be gathered from the fact that all animals fed upon the insects thrive when these are abundant; and the further fact that our locust-eating Indians, and all other locust-eating people, grow fat upon them.

". . . When freshly caught in large quantities, the mangled mass [of locusts] presents a not very appetizing appearance, and emits a rather strong and not over pleasant odor; but rinsed and scalded, they turn a brownish red, look much more inviting, and give no disagreeable smell. . . .

"Like or dislike of many kinds of food are very much matters of individual taste or national custom. Every nation has some special and favorite dish which the people of other nations will scarcely touch, while the very animal that is highly esteemed in one part of a country is not unfrequently rejected as poisonous in another section. We use many things to-day that were considered worthless or even poisonous by our forefathers. Prejudice wields a most powerful influence in all our actions. It is said that the Irish during the famine of 1857, would rather starve than eat corn-bread; and if what I have written shall, in the future, induce some of our Western people to profit by the hint, and avoid suffering from hunger or actual starvation, I shall not have written in vain."

SHARK

THE CLASSIC IMAGE of a shark is that of a vicious villain constantly plagued by hunger as it searches warm seas for small fish or even for a swimming man. Some sharks disprove this view, however. The 45-foot Whale Shark (*Rhincodon typus*), weighing up to 13 tons, restricts its dining to small fish, crustaceans, and plankton; it is the largest of all fish living today.

A shark is a primitive fish that has made few evolutionary changes in the past 300 million years. Its torpedo-shaped body has no true bones and is supported only by cartilage. Its tough gray skin is covered with small toothlike scales. Behind and below the snout is a savage mouth rimmed with formidable teeth. The tail is usually notched, with the upper extension longer than the lower.

The 20-foot Thresher Shark (*Alopias vulpinus*), weighing over 1,000 pounds, is found in all temperate seas. Its upper tail lobe is as long as its body. A thresher flails a school of small fish with its powerful tail before rapaciously scooping up masses of victims in its mouth. The flesh of a thresher is praised as good eating.

The 4-foot Spiny Dogfish (*Squalus acanthias*), weighing about 20 pounds, is a shark of northern oceans that is usually disregarded by Americans as a food, partly because more favored fish are available and partly because the dogfish damages so much fishing gear and destroys so many superior fish along the shorelines. The dogfish is an important food species in Europe, however, where it is often marketed under the name of grayfish. Euell Gibbons was not pleased with the results of baking, boiling, steaming, or broiling a dogfish but declared that strips he batter-fried in the English fish-and-chips manner were delicious, with a flavor reminiscent of lobster; he also produced good fish cakes with ground fillets.

The 6-foot Soupfin Shark (*Galaeorhinus zyopterus*) of California waters weighs up to 100 pounds. It yields a gelatinous fin, rich in protein and vitamins, which is prized for making soup. Its liver is valuable for its high content of vitamin A. A United States fishery leaflet compares kippered soupfin favorably to sablefish or salmon; the bulletin likens shark meat in general to that of swordfish.

To prepare shark's fin for eating, the golden pectoral (chest) fin requires soaking overnight followed by an hour or two of simmering. Both the gray dorsal (back) fin and the gray caudal (tail) fin require soaking for two or three days followed by several hours of simmering.

31

Ritual communion bowl depicting a *shark*.
From Santa Ana, Solomon Islands,
twentieth century.
Height 22.5 centimeters,
length 46.8 centimeters.
The University Museum,
Philadelphia, #67–5–3.

SHARK'S FIN SOUP

¼ pound dried golden shark's fin, without rough skin	Soak fin overnight in water to cover.
1 ham hock *2 chicken wings* *1 leek* *3 cups water*	Combine ham hock, chicken wings, leek, and water. Bring to boil, then simmer for 1 hour. Strain stock into clean container. Discard remaining ingredients. Chill stock until fat solidifies at top; discard fat.
1 leek *1-inch cube fresh ginger root* *¼ cup dried mushrooms broken into small pieces*	Drain fin, cover with fresh water, and simmer with leek and ginger for 1 hour. Rinse mushrooms, cover with warm water, and soak for 1 hour. Drain fin; discard leek and ginger. Tear fin into bite-sizes. Combine fins with ham/chicken stock and mushrooms/water; simmer for 45 minutes or until fins are soft.
1 tablespoon cornstarch *¼ cup cream sherry* *1 tablespoon soy sauce*	Combine cornstarch, sherry, and soy sauce. Add to soup and stir constantly until smoothly thickened. Serves 4.

SALMON

HIGH ABOVE THE WATERFALLS in narrow headwaters of a Pacific river, the female salmon thrashes her tail against a shallow gravelbottom to scoop a wide nesting place for eggs. The pink globules she lays are milted at once by her protective male. A few months later *alevina* hatch and hide unobtrusively for several weeks while nourished by yolk sacs attached to their stomachs. At last they become free-swimming little fish called *fry*. In about a year they mature into *fingerlings* or *parr*, leave their quiet upstream home, and journey downstream for many months in quest of larger-swimming food and salt water. Once they reach the sea they visit wondrous ocean bottoms, perhaps two thousand miles away, perhaps for periods as long as seven years. In time they yearn for native waters and with unerring navigation, instrumented by their sense of smell, return to the rivermouth of their birthplace. Leaping and struggling valiantly, they rise above turbulent rapids to tranquil nesting grounds. The males in particular undergo spectacular color changes during this climb. In battered raiment they spawn a new generation as did their parents before them, and then—responsibility to their lineage fulfilled—they fade and die. Thus, in essence, goes the life history of almost any salmon, one species varying from another mainly in size, time, and distance traveled.

The largest of all salmon, the King or Chinook (*Oncorhynchus tshawytscha*), may weigh from 18 to 100 pounds. During three or four years at sea it may be captured by a fisherman for its red, pink, or white savoury flesh. If the male succeeds in fighting his way to quiet headwaters, his silvery body with small black spots becomes a dull black with somber red blotches, and his jaw distorts with half-inch teeth.

The smallest and most numerous salmon is the Humpback or Pink (*O. gorbuscha*) weighing from 3 to 11 pounds. Inch-long fry descend to ocean waters in the spring and return a year from the following fall to spawn and die. As the male works his way upstream, a huge hump of cartilage develops on his back. When he reaches fresh water, his delicious pink flesh loses its flavor and attractiveness to man.

The salmon most prized for its red-orange flesh and outstanding flavor is the Sockeye (*O. nerka*) weighing from 5 to 15 pounds. The male, who is blue-green with black speckles during his two or three years at sea, acquires a bright red body with a greenish head as he makes his springtime run to spawning waters.

The greatest game fish in the world according to many anglers challenged by its speed, strength, and wiliness is the lively Atlantic Salmon (*Salmo salar*). Some Atlantics never leave fresh water; they have blackish-olive

ABOVE: Tlingit wooden spoon with *salmon* design, family crest of the owner. Used to whip soapberries into foam much liked as a dessert. Collected in Alaska before 1867. Length 13½ inches. Peabody Museum, Harvard University, Cambridge, #1721.

bodies with irregular black spots and weigh from 3 to 20 pounds. Others live at sea for perhaps five years before returning to fresh water to spawn, and some make three successful round trips from salt to spawning waters before dying. They have silver sides with blue-gray backs and black spots, and they weigh from 10 to 100 pounds.

SALMON, PICKLED

2 pounds center section of fresh, lean, red salmon

2 tablespoons salt

Carefully remove bones, skin, and fat from meat. Sprinkle salt over meat. Place whole fillets in glass container in refrigerator.

1 tablespoon dried, mixed pickling spices

Small square of cheesecloth

¼ cup white granulated sugar

¾ cup white distilled vinegar

¼ cup water

Tie pickling spices in cheesecloth. Combine spice packet, sugar, vinegar, and water in stainless steel or glass saucepan. Bring to boil, cover, simmer for 15 minutes, remove from heat, and cool thoroughly.

1 small white onion, sliced

1 large lemon, sliced and seeded

Pour cold brine over fish. Include spice packet. Cover with onion and lemon slices. Be sure all fish is completely immersed. Cover container. Refrigerate 48 hours, gently rotating fish a few times during that interval. Drain and cut meat into thin slices or ½-inch cubes. Garnish with parsley and freshly-sliced lemon, and serve as appetizer. Yield: about 2 cups.

Tlingit basket embroidered with a *salmon*.
From Alaska.
Height 6 inches, diameter 5¼ inches.
Courtesy of Charles Miles, Oakland.

Vicus stirrup-spout bottle of creamware ceramic in the form of a hawk standing on an *eel*. From Peru, 300–100 B.C. Height 8½ inches. Collection of Domingo Seminario Urrutia, Lima-Piura, Peru.

EEL

DEEP DOWN IN THE CLEAR BLUE WATERS of the warm Sargasso Sea, in the saltiest part of the North Atlantic, the female eel lays her eggs during the last months of the year. The following spring the larvae, called *leptocephali,* hatch in this sea that has no land boundaries. They grow into willow-leafed shapes about 3 inches long, so thin and transparent they seem more like eyeglasses than fish. Larvae spawned by an American Eel (*Anguilla rostrata*) are caught up in the Gulf Stream and a year later appear along American coastlines. Those spawned by a European Eel (*A. anguilla*) drift with the North Atlantic Current for almost three years before reaching the shores of Europe. Near the mouths of rivers the larvae take on the snakelike form of eels and acquire pigment in their bodies. Males remain in tidewaters. Female *elvers,* or young eels, swim upriver, sometimes as far as the headwaters, where they remain for six to eight years. When finally mature, the females return to salt water where they are joined by males and go back to the Sargasso Sea to spawn and die. A mature eel may measure 2 to 4 feet in length. Its serpentine body is covered with skin so smooth that tiny scales embedded in the slippery case barely can be detected. A continuous, spineless fin stretches from mid-stomach, along a centerline, around the tip of the vertically-flattened tail, then forward along the back to a point behind the head. There are no breast fins, and the gill openings are very small.

The largest catches of eels are made in rivers during the fall migration. Some are caught in wire traps called eelpots; others are netted, speared, or caught on setlines. The million-or-so pounds of eels shipped alive in fresh-water tanks to American markets every year are but a fraction of the number consumed abroad.

The predacious Moray Eel (*Gymnothorax moringa*) and the vicious Conger Eel (*Conger conger*) live their entire lifetimes in salt water. Though not appreciated for their personalities, they are nevertheless frequently enjoyed as food.

Eel meat contains considerable fat which is not fishy in flavor when properly prepared. Smoked eel is a special favorite in many countries.

To clean an eel, make a shallow cut through the skin, encircling the entire neck. Holding the head with a cloth, grasp the skin just below the neck-cut with a pair of pliers and strip off the skin, from neck to tail, like a glove. Slit the stomach from vent to throat. Discard the intestines as well as the head.

EELS BROILED, WITH LEMON SAUCE

4 fresh eels (about 1 pound each), skinned and beheaded

½ bay leaf

½ teaspoon salt

Water

Fillet each eel. Coil backbones in saucepan, add bay leaf, salt, and water to cover; simmer for ½ hour.

Place eel fillets, gray secondary-skin up, on uncovered baking pan. Place pan 6 inches below broiler heat. Broil eels 10 minutes. Peel off and discard gray skin. Turn over eels. Broil 5 more minutes. Place each eel on paper towel to blot oil. Serve on preheated plates with hot lemon sauce. Serves 4.

4 fresh large eggs

¼ cup lemon juice

½ cup eel stock made from backbones

Lemon sauce: Over low heat, beat eggs with wire whisk in top half of double boiler, with simmering water in lower half. Add lemon juice and continue beating. Slowly add hot eel stock and continue beating until sauce thickens. Do not overcook, or sauce will curdle. Serve at once.

36

Haida mat woven from spruce root, representing a *halibut*.
From Queen Charlotte Islands. Collected by Emmons in 1912.
Length about 8 inches.
Courtesy of the American Museum of Natural History, New York, #16/1/1195E.

HALIBUT

THE ANGUISHED FACE of a halibut conceivably could have inspired Picasso
to paint his distorted portrait of a lady with two front-view eyes staring
from a side-view profile. Until the translucent larva of a halibut grows to a
length of about one inch, it looks like a conventional fish that anyone might
have painted. Then its left eye shifts upward toward its right eye, its mouth
twists to a horizontal plane, its left side turns toward the ocean bottom and
takes on white pigment, and its darkening right side usurps the topside as
king-of-the-hill. Thus the halibut transforms itself from a vertical fish into a
flat fish and takes on the characteristics of its kinsfolk the flounders, the
soles, and the turbots. And thus the halibut comes to look like a sculpture
that might have come from the hands of Picasso.

37

The Atlantic Halibut (*Hippoglossus hippoglossus*) grows to a length of 9 feet and a weight of 700 pounds, although 300 pounds is a more likely figure today. A female grows to a length of 1 foot in about 3 years and 6 feet in about 20 years; she becomes much larger than a male and may live to be 40 years old. The Pacific Halibut (*H. stenolepis*) reaches 9 feet in length and 500 pounds in weight. The Atlantic species suffered severely from overfishing which prompted conservation measures that saved the Pacific species from a similar fate.

The smooth-scaled halibut lives near the bottom of cold—but not arctic—waters, feeding on smaller fishes, squids, and crabs. Hungry sharks and seals are its mortal enemies. Fishermen catch halibut with trawls or with hooks tied a few feet apart on longlines in waters as deep as 3,600 feet.

The mild, firm, white flesh of the halibut deserves man's eternal blessing. Indeed, the very name halibut derives from Middle English *haly butte*, meaning holy flatfish—food to be eaten by Christians on holy days. Especially succulent meat comes from chicken-halibut which weigh less than 20 pounds.

HALIBUT CASSEROLE WITH BROCCOLI, CHEESE, AND CHIPS

10 ounces (about 2½ cups) frozen chopped broccoli

Unwrap and thaw broccoli on towel so excess moisture will be absorbed.

3 tablespoons butter
3 tablespoons flour
¼ teaspoon salt
¼ teaspoon white pepper
1 cup milk

Melt butter in top half of double boiler, with simmering water in lower half. Add flour, salt, and pepper; heat for 5 minutes, stirring with wire whisk. Add milk; heat for 20 minutes, stirring occasionally.

2 pounds fresh halibut
½ pound sharp cheddar cheese, diced
5 ounces potato chips

Remove bone and skin from halibut; cut meat into 1-inch chunks. In large bowl, combine halibut, cheese, somewhat-crumbled potato chips, broccoli, and white sauce. Pour into oiled casserole (about 7"x12"x2".) Cover. Bake in preheated 350°F oven for 35 minutes. Serves 6 to 8.

FROG

FISHES THAT FIRST VENTURED FROM THE OCEAN and tried to live on land became extinct as species long ago. A few descendants, however, changed their ways appreciably and thus survive as amphibians today, able to live on land but still very dependent on the water. Frogs are among those few. It remained for the reptiles to be the first vertebrates to completely free themselves of water and truly conquer land.

Frogs of the genus *Rana* occur throughout most of the world except Australia. The Bullfrog (*Rana catesbeiana*) is the largest frog in the United States. Its black-and-white eggs lack a protective shell; surrounded only by a jelly-like covering, they must be laid in fresh water. In five to twenty days they hatch into vegetable-eating tadpoles equipped with gills for breathing and a tail for swimming. In about two years gills and tail are replaced by lungs and legs, and diet changes to insects, earthworms, minnows, and crayfish. In another four years the bullfrog matures to a length of 6 to 8 inches and weighs up to 5 pounds. A few live to the age of 15 years. Because of long, muscular hind legs, the web-footed bullfrog can leap on land as far as six feet in one jump, the landing shock being absorbed by its short front legs. It prefers to spend most of its time in ponds and slow streams, however, and retreats to soft mud under the water during winter hibernation. A bullfrog's smooth, greenish skin lacks scales and is usually moist. Throughout the warmest nights of summer the male bullfrog serenades his soft-spoken females with a deep-voiced song, *jug-o-rummmm*.

Gourmets compete with biology students when it comes to frogs. In this country only the legs of a frog are marketed for food, but the diner must sustain the cost of the entire frog because he is competing with a biology student who is willing to pay a good price for every inch of the animal he studies in the classroom. In 1938 the wholesale price for bullfrogs was less than three cents a pound; in 1974 the price was at least eighty-five cents a pound, reflecting the rising demand in high cuisine as well as in science and also indicating the diminishing supply of frogs in general as civilization encroaches on wetlands where frogs once thrived. Over 1,260 tons of frogs were sold for frogs' legs in Louisiana in 1936; less than 21 tons were sold in 1967. Frogs' legs are imported from France where for decades they have been bred and fattened for the epicure. Many frogs' legs also come from Japan and India. Their flavor is rather like chicken, but with a lighter, special quality.

Smaller frogs in the United States also prized as food are the Leopard or Grass Frog (*R. pipiens*) which has black leopard-like spots on its green back and the Green or Spring Frog (*R. clamitans*).

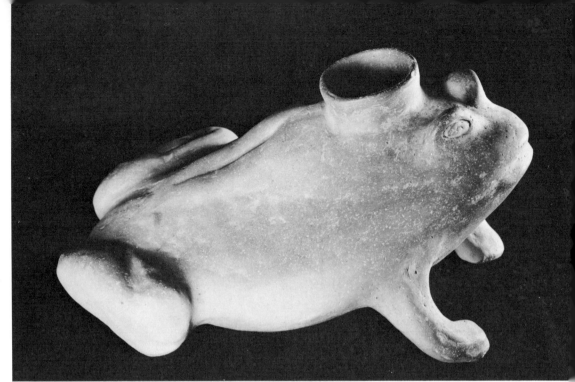

Ceramic vessel
in the form of a *frog*,
made by Mound Builder Indian,
about fourteenth century.
Found in Arkansas.
Length 12 inches.
Courtesy of The Denver Art Museum,
#XMB–28.

FROGS' LEGS, BATTER-FRIED WITH DILL

1½ pounds frogs' legs

½ cup dry white wine

½ cup water

2 sprigs fresh parsley

6 shoots fresh chives

⅛ teaspoon ground white pepper

Skin the legs and remove the feet. Cut legs apart at backbone. In glass loaf dish, combine wine, water, parsley, chives, pepper, and frogs' legs. Refrigerate for 2 hours, shifting ingredients a few times during that period. Drain and dry meat thoroughly.

2 large eggs

½ cup ice water

2 tablespoons flour

2 tablespoons cornstarch

½ teaspoon salt

Prepare batter just before using it; do not store in advance. Lightly beat eggs and water in chilled bowl. Stir in flour, cornstarch, and salt.

Pan containing safflower or peanut oil to a depth of 1½ inches

4 large sprigs fresh dill

Heat oil to 375°F. Dip legs in batter and deep-fry for 2 to 4 minutes, depending on size of leg. Drain on paper. Dip dill sprigs in batter and deep-fry until golden. Drain on paper. Garnish each serving of frogs' legs with sprig of dill. Serves 4.

TURTLE

OVER 200 MILLION YEARS AGO, before the dinosaurs appeared, the first turtles began roaming the earth. By most definitions a *tortoise* is a turtle that lives on land or in fresh water, and a *terrapin* is an edible turtle that lives in brackish or fresh water; a *turtle* may be either of the above or may be a turtle that lives in the sea. Being a reptile, a turtle has lungs for breathing air. Being a reptile, it also is cold-blooded, which means its body temperature is always about the same as its surroundings and it must therefore hibernate in the ground or in water in order to survive cold winters.

A turtle's squat body is covered by a dry, oval upper shell (carapace) and lower shell (plastron) which are formed by irregularly-shaped plates. Vertebrae and ribs are fused to these plates. Each year a new and larger scale grows under an old plate. The age of a young terrapin can be estimated by counting the rings of its horny plates, but rings are not a reliable measure of the age of an old one—especially some species' patriarchs that have lived more than 150 years. When retreating from danger or when sleeping, a turtle draws its head, legs, and tail between its two shells. A turtle cuts and rips its food with a toothless, horny beak. The female is usually larger than the male. She digs a nest in a sandy shore above the high-water mark, lays her clutch of eggs, covers them, and departs, never to recognize as her own offspring the young turtles that are eventually hatched by the warm sun.

A marine species with very savory flesh—rather like beef in color and texture and even in flavor—is the plant-eating Green Turtle (*Chelonia mydas*). It has a flattish, green carapace, and its fat also has a green tint. This flipper-limbed sea animal grows to a length of 4 feet and weighs as much as 400 pounds. Conservation efforts are under way in the Caribbean to save it from extinction.

Another turtle highly prized for its flesh is the Diamondback Terrapin (*Malaclemys terrapin*). It, too, is becoming rare and is protected by law in some states. This web-footed, short-legged reptile lives in brackish or salt water, feeding on plants, mollusks, and shellfish. Its arched carapace is brownish green with dark, angular rings around its plates, and its sides and flat plastron are yellow with black dots. In 1911, Artemas Ward wrote, "Within the last half century the Diamondback has developed from almost a waste product—an article fed to slaves and apprentices before the Civil War—to one of the highest priced of food delicacies." Today a terrapin raised at a commercial rearing station attains a length of 8 inches and a weight of 2 pounds in about 9 years.

The snapping turtle, the soft-shelled turtle, and the chicken turtle are also popular for eating.

Footed bowl of fired clay portraying a *turtle*
with a man's head in its mouth.
From British Honduras. Pre-Columbian.
Peabody Museum, Harvard University, Cambridge, #C/10376.

TURTLE GUMBO

1 smoked pork hock	Cover hock with water. Add parsley, onion, and
5 cups water	pepper. Bring to boil, cover, and simmer for 2
2 sprigs fresh parsley	hours. Strain broth; reserve. Discard remaining
1 small white onion, peeled	ingredients.
½ teaspoon dried crushed red pepper	
½ cup white flour	In large enamel-coated cast-iron pot, over low
3 tablespoons vegetable oil	heat, toss and stir flour until it becomes tan but
3 tablespoons butter	not scorched. Remove ¼ cup flour; reserve. To
6 small white onions	remaining ¼ cup flour, add oil and butter; blend.
	Add onions; stir and simmer a few minutes.

½ teaspoon dried thyme	Combine ¼ cup flour (reserved above) with thyme in paper bag. Cut meat into bite-size pieces. Blot the meat dry with towel. Shake meat in bag. Add to pot. Over high heat, sauté meat until brown. Add hock broth, cover, simmer for 2½ hours, stirring occasionally.
2 pounds fresh, lean sea turtle meat	
1 cup long-grain white rice	Cook rice according to directions on page 3.
2 cups water	
1 tablespoon butter	
½ teaspoon salt	
6 small hen's eggs	Gently lower eggs into boiling water to cover. Boil on medium-low heat for 15 minutes. Remove at once to bowl of water with ice cubes. Tap surface of each egg all over with flat knife handle to shatter shell; remove shell, being careful not to split egg white. Reserve eggs.
1½ cups (5 ounces) fresh or frozen baby okra	Cut okra crosswise into ½-inch sections. Reserve.
3 cups cherry tomatoes	Dip tomatoes into boiling water; immerse in cold water. Remove stems and skins. Reserve.
3 large stalks celery	Cut celery into bite-size pieces. Reserve.
1 tablespoon Worcestershire sauce	Twenty minutes before serving, add Worcestershire sauce, salt, and okra to simmering pot. Ten minutes before serving, add eggs. Five minutes before serving, add sherry, tomatoes, and celery. Just before serving, with broth at boiling point, remove pot from heat. Stir in filé powder.
½ teaspoon salt	
¼ cup dry sherry	
1½ teaspoons gumbo filé powder	
Tabasco sauce	For each serving, pack ½-cup measuring-cup with hot cooked rice and invert in center of wide soup bowl. Surround rice with meat, vegetables, egg, and broth. Pass Tabasco sauce at table for individual use. Serves 6.

Detail of *crocodile's head* on wooden bowl.
From Timbunke village, Middle-Sepik, New Guinea.
Height 9 centimeters, length 60 centimeters.
Courtesy of Museum voor Land- en Volkenkunde,
Rotterdam, Netherlands, #51802.

ALLIGATOR

THE CLOSEST LIVING RELATIVES of the dinosaurs that dominated the world
during most of the Age of Reptiles are the sluggish crocodilians. There are
four members of this surviving group: crocodiles, alligators, gavials, and
caymans. They are little changed from the time they first appeared during
the middle of that reptilian era and are little different from one another.
The backs of their cigar-shaped bodies and long tails are protected with
bony or horny plates. They spend most of their time in water, preferring
large bodies of shallow water and maintaining water holes as lairs that are
approachable only by underwater tunnels. They swim by lashing their
powerful tails from side to side while holding their web-footed legs against
their bodies. They can float in water with their bodies submerged so that
little more than their bulbous eyes and nostrils protrude into the air. When
they make excursions to land, they do not crawl, but walk on short, bowed
legs with their torsos well off the ground. These crocodilians feed on small
aquatic and shore animals, bolting their captive whole if it is no larger
than a duck and whiplashing larger prey in their jaws with sudden lurches
that tear the victims into smaller pieces. In winter they bury themselves in
mud or retreat quiescently to underwater holes. The female lays her clutch
of eggs in a nest built of mud and plants; because she is cold-blooded she
must depend on the heat of decaying nest materials and the sun to hatch
her offspring. She fiercely guards this egg mound until each hatchling
breaks through its tough, leathery shell by means of a special egg-tooth.

44

The crocodile has a long snout that tapers to a point. Its body is thinner and more agile than an alligator's, and its personality is more aggressive. It sometimes attacks large animals, including dogs, cows, or men. The extra-large fourth tooth in its lower jaw slips into a groove outside the upper jaw and is visible when the mouth is closed. Some crocodiles have a preference for salt water. When crocodiles make a weeping sound and produce large tears by crying, they are not expressing sorrow but rather are ridding their bodies of excess salt through special glands in the head. Africa, Asia, Australia, and the Americas all have crocodiles. In this country the American Crocodile (*Crocodylus acutus*) is found only in southern Florida today and rarely exceeds 12 feet in length.

The alligator has a short, broad snout that is rounded on the end. The large fourth tooth of its lower jaw fits into a pocket inside the upper jaw. An alligator prefers fresh water and likes to bask in the sun on a bank. The American Alligator (*Alligator mississippiensis*) is found in coastal areas from the Carolinas to Texas and is about 10 feet long.

Because crocodiles and alligators were overhunted for their tough skins that made valuable leathers and because many of their swamplands were drained for human use, the survival of these animals became critical a few years ago and they were put on the world list of rare and endangered species. In 1972 and 1973 carefully-controlled experimental harvests were permitted in Cameron Parish, Louisiana, because the state's alligator population had revived to more than 250,000. A harvest did not take place in 1974. A federal treaty prohibits the sale of alligator meat.

Pre-Columbian pottery bowl and *alligator* lid, from Filadelfia, Costa Rica.
Height 11½ inches, width 4¾ inches.
Yale University Art Gallery, New Haven; gift of Mr. and Mrs. Fred Olsen.

45

Carved wooden lid illustrating a proverb that stresses the difference of status between a *crocodile* (chief) and a *gavial* (commoner). The two reptiles are separated by a three-pointed coffin associated with Woyo aristocracy. Collected by I. Mesmaekers in Cabinda before 1956. Diameter 7½ inches. Copyright, Musée Royal de l'Afrique Centrale, Tervuren, Belgium, #56.88.1.

ALLIGATOR ACCORDING TO EXPERTS

In *Foods America Gave the World*, A. Hyatt Verrill describes the meat of the tail of a young alligator (from 3 to 6 feet long) as clear white, flaky, and delicate, so similar to a fillet of flounder in appearance and taste that few persons distinguish one from the other.

Some people compare the flavor of an alligator's tail to that of frogs' legs.

In *Gun Club Cook Book*, Charles Browne admonishes a cook not to tell his guests they're eating alligator until after they've finished.

Back in the days when alligators were plentiful in Florida, Marjorie Kinnan Rawlings in *Cross Creek Cookery* extolled the alligator as truly delicious. She cautioned that alligator—like liver or veal, which she said it resembled in texture and coloring—had to be cooked either very quickly or else a very long time, because in between it toughened. She suggested cutting cross-sections between the vertebrae, rolling them in seasoned flour, and frying quickly in butter. Or browning in butter, adding hot water and lemon juice, then simmering for two or more hours until tender.

As to crocodiles, Alexander Lake in *Hunter's Choice* prefers the legs but allows that shoulder steaks are also desirable. He explains that the musk glands of the neck are the offensive portions. To prepare the meat, he suggests by way of his friend F. Robinson that one broil thin slices of crocodile, add sweet red wine, ginger, and salt to the resulting brown sauce, pour the liquid over the meat, top with grated cheese and butter, bake in a fast oven until browned, and serve with sautéed sliced mushrooms.

Pre-Columbian ceramic vessel in the form of an *iguana*, with mouth spout. Length 20 inches. Courtesy of The Art Institute of Chicago, #67.722.

IGUANA

THE DRAGON-LIKE APPEARANCE of the iguana makes an awesome portrait when enlarged by a science-fiction cameraman. Those initiated in the ways of this reptile, however, know it to be a timid and slow-witted lizard easily captured by man. It does not devour beautiful blond film actresses but instead feeds daintily on tender green leaves seasoned with occasional small insects. The bright green Common Iguana (*Iguana iguana*) of tropical America has a long black-banded tail, a spiny crest along its backbone, and a floppy bag under its throat. It grows to a length of 6 feet. Trees are its favorite clubhouse, especially those with riverside branches that serve as convenient springboards for diving into pools. It swims well by wriggling its body without using its four squatty legs and long-digited feet.

The iguana is hunted for its scaly hide as well as for its delicate white flesh which is likened to chicken and is commonly sold in tropical American markets. Eggs of the iguana are highly esteemed.

Relatives of this iguana which are also enjoyed as food in warm areas of the world include the chuckwalla and the spiny iguana of Mexico and Central America, the marine iguana of the Galapagos Islands, the goanna of Australia and Africa, and many other lizards of the Old World.

IGUANA MOLÉ

3 pounds iguana meat

Boiling water

Juice of 1 large lime

Cover iguana meat with boiling water in kettle to which lime juice has been added. Simmer for 30 minutes, or until tender. Tear meat into long, slender strips. Reserve stock.

1 pound fresh sweet green peppers

1 medium onion, quartered

2 cloves garlic, minced

2 tablespoons vegetable oil

½ tablespoon crushed dried hot red peppers, or more, according to taste

Cut green peppers into quarters; discard seeds and stems. Place quarters—skin side up—on tray under broiler until skins blister; peel off skins; place in blender. Add onion and garlic. Purée. In flameproof earthenware pot, over low heat on stovetop, combine oil, red peppers, and blender mixture. Simmer, stirring occasionally with wooden spoon, while preparing other ingredients.

1½ pounds fresh tomatoes

1 large tortilla, toasted and crumbled

¼ cup seedless raisins

¾ cup ground almonds

½ teaspoon salt

¼ teaspoon anise seed

¼ teaspoon ground cloves

¼ teaspoon ground cinnamon

1 ounce unsweetened chocolate

Plunge tomatoes in boiling water for about a minute; remove skins; cut in half—crosswise—and press out seeds; cut halves into sections and place in blender. Add tortilla, raisins, almonds, salt, anise, cloves, and cinnamon. Purée. Add to earthenware pot. Cut chocolate into slivers over pot. Add 1 cup stock. Simmer 1 hour, thinning with additional stock if desired.

16 large tortillas

4 tablespoons sesame seeds

Wrap tortillas tightly in aluminum foil and heat in preheated 325° oven for 20 minutes. Likewise heat meat in tightly-covered dish. Serve meat and molé on hot tortillas, sprinkled with sesame seeds. Serve with cactus salad and refried beans. Serves 8.

Colima ceramic vessel
in the form of a coiled *rattlesnake*.
From west coast of Mexico,
A.D. 100–400.
Length 7 inches.
Courtesy of The Art Institute of Chicago.

RATTLESNAKE

ONE OF THE DEADLIEST SNAKES in the world is the Diamondback Rattle-snake (*Crotalus adamanteus*) of the southeastern coast of the United States. Olive and yellow scales form a pattern of diamonds along the back of this dry, smooth creature that crawls among palmettos and low, sandy brushlands. An average 6-foot adult weighs from 12 to 15 pounds. Its 3-inch-wide head has a deep pit in front of each eye. As a rattler's scales enlarge, its outer skin must be cast off so a larger covering can replace it. The snake splits through its hood and then wiggles away, leaving the old, translucent coat behind, turned inside-out. The snake's lidless eyes never close and are protected by rigid, transparent eyecaps which are shed along with the rest of the skin. A rattlesnake may molt two to four times a year, adding a new hollow ring at the end of its tail after each molting. Some of the outermost rattle rings break away on older snakes. A diamondback may or may not sound a warning by shaking these loose, horny tail rings before striking with its fangs which are hollow teeth in its upper jaw and which carry paralyzing venom from ducts behind the eyes into the skin of a vic-tim. For an interval after a rattlesnake's head has been severed from its body, it is capable of biting and poisoning an adversary. The slender, forked tongue of this viper is not an instrument for delivering poison but is a smelling aid that picks up tiny particles from the ground and deposits them in a smelling organ in the roof of the mouth. A rattlesnake hears by feeling ground vibrations through its body rather than by picking up sound waves from the air. A rattler's favorite food is live rabbit or quail, swallowed

whole. It can survive more than a year without food but normally eats at more or less regular intervals and develops much fat within the muscles that cushion its 200-or-so vertebrae. As a cold-blooded reptile, a rattlesnake must hibernate in winter; during extremely hot weather it must estivate or retreat to the protection of inner ground. Springtime is its most active period. A litter of 8 to 12 young is born alive (not hatched from eggs) in August or September. Each offspring is a little over a foot long and is immediately able to take care of all its needs—which means it can bite with virulence. About twenty-eight species of rattlesnakes thrive in America.

Rattlesnake oil has been sought since ancient times as a sovereign cure for a staggering variety of ills, including rheumatism, backache, toothache, sore throat, gout, goiter, and frostbite.

Rattlesnake meat has served as ritual food in Indian tribal ceremonies and as emergency ration for pioneers out of provisions. The animal is easily captured by someone weakened by starvation. The best time to hunt it is in the autumn when it is fattest.

Any prejudice a novice eater may have against a rattlesnake because of its appearance or personality is usually overcome when the meat is tasted. Chroniclers over three centuries have compared the flavor to eel, canned tuna, frog, tortoise, chicken, quail, opossum, or rabbit. Rattlesnake meat has appeared on menus as "prairie eel." A 4-foot rattlesnake yields 1 pound of meat; 5-foot, 2½ pounds; 6-foot, 4½ pounds; 7-foot, 7½ pounds; 8-foot, 11½ pounds.

When properly cooked, the enormous boa and anaconda of tropical America are considered superior to rattlesnake. Recipes from Africa and India recommend that a python be curried. Natives of Australia consider as disconcerting the haphazard shapes that result from broiling a snake untended. Therefore, two cooks stretch a snake over a campfire to eliminate distortions of form and also to keep juices in the flesh; then they roll the snake like a pinwheel, tie it together with reeds, insulate it with ashes, and bake it in hot coals.

Ashanti wooden spoon with carvings of two *snakes* forming the handle.
From African Gold Coast, 1900–1914. Length 20 inches.
Náprstek Museum, Prague, Czechoslovakia, #25.559.

RATTLESNAKE MMMMMMMMM!

2 fresh rattlesnakes, about 2 pounds after skinning and beheading

½ cup corn meal

½ teaspoon salt

¼ cup bacon fat

¼ teaspoon Tabasco sauce

Cut bodies crosswise into 2-inch sections. Roll meat in mixture of cornmeal and salt. Combine bacon fat and Tabasco sauce in large skillet. Sauté meat until brown and tender. Serves 3.

OSTRICH

WHEN REPTILES CEASED TO DOMINATE THE WORLD about sixty-five million years ago, the ostrich evolved as a bird resembling the ancient dinosaur that walked on hind legs. Like that horny reptile, the ostrich had scales on its legs and feet. Unlike that cold-blooded creature, however, the ostrich was warm-blooded and not entirely dependent on its surroundings to maintain a constant body temperature. The ostrich acquired feathers but lost the skill to fly. It relies on long, strong legs instead of ineffective wings to speed it to its goal. If a wary ostrich panics at the sign of a hunter, it runs in a large circle, perhaps as fast as thirty-five miles an hour. When cornered, it defends itself by kicking and slashing viciously with its two-toed feet, the largest toes having awesome nails as thick as elephant bullets. Cave paintings in Herschel, South Africa, show bushmen wearing ostrich skins and holding the animals' heads aloft on long neck-sticks as they stalk the live birds with bows and arrows.

The African Ostrich (*Struthio camelus*) is the largest bird living in the world today. It stands about 8 feet high and weighs up to 345 pounds. The rangy neck and small head of the male are covered with pinkish down while the glossy black feathers of his body are accented with luxurious white plumes on his tail and wings. The hen ostrich, who is feathered in a monotone of dull gray, sits inconspicuously on her clutch of a dozen or so eggs during the day. At night the cock takes his turn warming the nest, which is no more than a hollow scratched in the sand. Each ivory egg measures about 5 inches in diameter and 6 inches in length and weighs about 3 pounds. The ostrich produces the largest egg of any bird living today. The largest egg ever found, having almost six times the volume of an ostrich egg, came from the *Aepyornis*, an extinct bird of Madagascar thought by some to be the fabulous Roc that carried off Sinbad the Sailor in *Arabian Nights* and called by others the Elephant Bird because—it is said— it lifted elephants to its nest to feed its young.

On the wild, arid plains of Africa, ostriches live gregariously in flocks of ten to fifty, conversing with each other in booming roars and piercing hisses. They amicably coexist with giraffes and antelopes, serving as watchtowers for the entire herd, their farsighted, eyelashed eyes ever alert to danger. Ostriches feed on grasses, seeds, and fruits and occasionally on insects, small reptiles, and birds. Domesticated ostriches on farms in Australia, Argentina, and southern Africa fare well on alfalfa and grain. Men have trained ostriches to pull carts, but as draft animals they tire easily and then balkily fold their legs down to the ground.

At an extravagant banquet in ancient Rome the profligate emperor Heliogabalus (A.D. 218–222) offered the brains of six hundred ostriches as special enticement to the pleasures of his guests. In the seventh century the noted physician Paulus of Aegina was well known for favoring the flesh of ostrich wings as an especially toothsome repast. The French naturalist Baron Cuvier (1769–1832) often partook of ostrich eggs and found them very delicate. About an hour is required to hard-boil an ostrich egg. In recent times in African markets the dried flesh of ostrich has been sold as biltong, and dehydrated ostrich eggs have also been available.

OSTRICH EGG WITH CURRY SAUCE

1 cup sour cream

1 tablespoon Madras curry powder

1 tablespoon poppy seeds

Combine sour cream, curry powder, and poppy seeds in top of double boiler. Heat over simmering water while preparing eggs.

1 ostrich egg or 9 large hen's eggs (=2 cups, before beating)

¾ cup cold chicken stock

2 tablespoons dry vermouth

½ teaspoon salt

Vegetable oil

Combine eggs, chicken stock, vermouth, and salt. Beat until blended but not frothy. Strain through a coarse sieve. Brush bottom and sides of heavy 10-inch skillet with oil and place over medium heat. Using ladle with 3-tablespoon capacity, dip 3 tablespoons egg mixture into skillet. Rotate and tilt pan so egg spreads flat as quickly as possible. As soon as egg is cooked, remove pan from heat and roll egg into a cylindrical shape against one edge of skillet. Again brush bottom and sides of skillet with oil. Repeat ladling and cooking, as above. Roll first egg cylinder over second egg pancake to opposite side of skillet. Repeat oiling/frying/rolling cylinders to opposite sides of pan twice more. Remove omelet to preheated plate. Make 3 more omelets, as above.

1 tablespoon fresh chives, chopped

Spoon hot curry sauce over each omelet. Sprinkle chives over each serving. Serves 4.

For thousands of years the thick, pitted shell of an ostrich egg has been valued by men as a receptacle for food. In Mesopotamia ostrich-egg cups have been found in Sumerian graves dated 3000 B.C. Ancient Egyptians, Chinese, and Greeks used the shells as important objects of trade. Early bushmen in South Africa removed the contents of an egg through a small hole, filled the shell with water, stoppered the canteen with grass, and cached a large number for use in times of drought; they sometimes pecked designs onto the shells with a sharp stone and also made polished beads from broken shards.

Ostrich-egg goblet with silver mounts and with gold *ostrich* on cover.
Made in Prague, about 1570.
Trustees of the British Museum, London.

53

GOOSE

WATERFOWL WERE AMONG THE FIRST birds that man tried to domesticate. The common barnyard goose of today is descended from the Graylag Goose (*Anser anser*) which still lives by its own guile in the uninhabited reaches of northern Europe and Asia. The tame goose has all but lost its ability to fly, but each autumn and spring the wild graylag makes long migratory flights on wide, powerful wings between the cold marshlands of the arctic and the warm, hospitable retreats edging the Mediterranean.

As middleman among its kinsfolk, a goose is smaller than a swan and larger than a duck. Its neck is shorter than that of the graceful swan and longer than that of a duck. A goose proudly holds its neck straight upward when swimming and stretches it due forward when flying in V-formation with other members of its flock. It swims well with its webbed feet but is not as aquatically inclined as a swan. It walks more effectively on land than either a swan or a duck because it has longer legs positioned advantageously in the center of its body. A goose's beak serves as a hand as well as a mouth—enabling it to gather grains and insects for food, to defend itself from attackers, to waterproof its coat by rubbing oil from a tail gland onto its feathers, and to weave a ground nest of reeds and line it with down. The male goose, called a gander, chooses a female as a lifetime mate and conscientiously shares the responsibilities of raising their young offspring, called goslings.

The honking Canada Goose (*Branta canadensis*) is the most common wild goose in North America today. It varies from 25 to 43 inches in length and weighs up to 13 pounds. The grayish body of both the male and female is distinguished by a black neck and head and by a wide, white chin-band stretching from cheek to cheek.

There are fourteen species of geese in the world today. For culinary purposes, their dark flesh offers all gradations of flavor and texture. Wild birds are improved by hanging for several days, and as there is little fat on their bodies they usually require generous larding and basting while roasting. Domestic geese, on the other hand, are noteworthy for their excessive fat; the rendered fat is treasured by many cooks for special uses in the kitchen. A young goose with a pliant underbill is more tender than an oldster with a worn, rigid bill. A goose raised commercially for the table is typically marketed at the age of 10 weeks when it weighs about 14 pounds. A bird more than 6 months old may require special strategy and patience in cooking.

Bronze vessel in the shape of a *goose*.
From China, Chou dynasty, about 300 B.C.
Height 9½ inches, length 16¼ inches.
The Minneapolis Institute of Arts, #62.71.1.

55

GOOSE STUFFED WITH CHESTNUTS AND PRUNES

30 fresh chestnuts

With tip of paring knife, gash a small "x" through shell of each chestnut. Cover chestnuts with water in saucepan, bring to boil, and simmer for a few minutes. Remove one chestnut at a time, and while it is still warm, remove shell and *all* the bitter skin. In small saucepan, cover peeled chestnuts with water, bring to boil, and simmer for ½ hour.

30 large pitted prunes

Stuff each prune with a chestnut, sealing prune tightly around chestnut.

8-pound domestic goose
2 teaspoons salt

Dry the goose, inside and out. Rub with salt, inside and out. Place stuffed prunes inside goose. Close openings by sewing or skewering; tie legs and wings close to body. Prick small holes in skin to permit excess fat to escape; repeat pricking occasionally during roasting. Place goose, breast up, in uncovered roasting pan in preheated 425°F oven for 20 minutes. As roasting progresses, siphon off excess fat with bulb-baster and transfer fat to tall jar. Reduce heat to 350°F. Allow 20 minutes per pound roasting time. Goose is done when leg moves easily in its socket. Remove goose to preheated platter and keep warm.

1 tablespoon cornstarch
¼ cup Madeira wine

Ladle off excess fat from drippings; add enough water to drippings to equal 1 cup liquid. Combine cornstarch with Madeira; blend with drippings. Over medium heat, stir until sauce is thickened, but do not boil. Serve hot sauce and stuffed prunes as accompaniment to goose. Serves 6.

DUCK

WITH SHORT LEGS AFT OF CENTER, a duck waddles awkwardly on dry land. In water, however, this leg design coupled with webbed feet enables the bird to swim and dive swiftly and skillfully. In most of the eighty-or-so species of ducks in the world, the male, called a drake, has plumage that is bold and colorful compared to the drab wrappings of the female, called a hen. Only during the annual molt when loss of feathers prohibits flying does the male wear a dull coat as he hides out until his new feathers become long and dense. The flat bill of most ducks has saw-toothed edges that are useful in grasping and straining food. No present-day birds have actual teeth.

Most domestic ducks are descendants of the Mallard Duck (*Anas platyrhynchos*) which is a "dipping" duck and is the most abundant wild waterfowl in the northern hemisphere today. A white collar separates the male's glossy green head and neck from his brownish body. Each wing bears a badge of blue edged with bars of black and white, the only bold-colored identification that does not neutralize to dead-grass tones during his molt. His orange webbed feet lack the flap on the hind toes that is characteristic of most ducks. A mallard forages in shallow waters for plants, mollusks, and insects by dipping its yellow bill deep down while its body floats vertically and its tail points to the clouds. It grows to a length of 20 to 28 inches. The female lays her eggs in a ground nest built of grass and lined with down plucked from her breast. The white Pekin duck of ancient mallard lineage was imported to this country from China in 1890 and is now our most important domestic duck. Long Island roaster ducklings marketed at the age of 8 or 9 weeks weigh from 4 to 5½ pounds.

The vegetable-feeding Canvasback Duck (*Aythya valisineria*), a "diving" duck, is a favorite of sportsmen in North America. The male's ash-colored body is distinguished by a rusty head and neck with a wide black bib around his upper chest. His forehead slopes gradually into a long black bill. A 20- to 24-inch bird weighs up to 3 pounds.

The Wood Duck (*Aix sponsa*) of North America and the Mandarin Duck (*A. galericulata*) of eastern Asia are closely-related "perching" ducks. They nest in tree hollows and spend a good deal of time on tree limbs, aided by feet that are clawed as well as webbed and are strengthened with a powerful hind toe. The 20-inch males are feathered brightly in contrast to the sombre females.

Many sportsmen adamantly insist that a plucked, properly-hung wild duck should be roasted plain—untouched inside or outside by seasonings, stuffings, or sauces—in a *very* hot oven for only 15 minutes, or at the most 20 minutes if the specimen is large.

Bronze cooking vessel with handle in the form of a *duck's head*.
From China, Han dynasty, 206 B.C.–A.D. 220. Height 7 inches.
Trustees of the British Museum, London; Eumorfopoulos collection.

The Bombay Duck which appears on shelves of gourmet shops is not a duck at all but a 16-inch phosphorescent fish, the Bunmallow (*Harpodon nehereus*) from the estuaries of northern India. It is dried and tinned in Bombay. The flavor of the fish is quite transformed when toasted over a flame. It can be munched as an hors d'oeuvre or crumbled into a curry.

58

DUCK WITH ALMONDS AND PRESERVED GINGER

5-pound domestic duck

2 tablespoons soy sauce

Juice pressed from 1 clove garlic

½ teaspoon salt

⅛ teaspoon white pepper

Blot duck dry with clean towel. Combine soy sauce, garlic juice, salt, and pepper. Rub mixture into duck surfaces, inside and outside. Prick small holes in skin to permit fat to escape; repeat pricking periodically during roasting. Place duck, breast down, on uncovered shallow roasting pan in preheated 450°F oven; roast for 15 minutes. Reduce heat to 325°F. Turn duck on its side and roast for 30 minutes. Turn duck on its other side and roast for 30 minutes. Turn duck on its back and roast for 30 minutes. Siphon or ladle off fat and juices accumulated in pan; reserve them in tall, slender jar.

¼ cup syrup from preserved ginger bulbs

¼ cup dry white wine

2 tablespoons rice vinegar

Siphon or ladle off fat from dark juices in jar. To juices, add ginger syrup, wine, and vinegar. With this mixture baste duck frequently during remaining roasting time of about 1 hour and 15 minutes. Duck is done when leg moves easily in its socket. Remove duck to warming platter for carving.

1 tablespoon cornstarch

2 tablespoons dry white wine

⅓ cup blanched, sliced almonds

6 ginger bulbs preserved in syrup, each bulb about ½ inch diameter & sliced crosswise into thin discs

Pour pan drippings through strainer. Siphon or ladle off excess fat. Reduce juices by boiling, or add water—whichever is necessary to produce 1 cup stock. Combine cornstarch and wine, add to hot stock, and stir over low heat until smoothly thickened; do not boil. Add almonds and ginger. Spoon hot sauce over each serving of duck. Serve with rice. Serves 4.

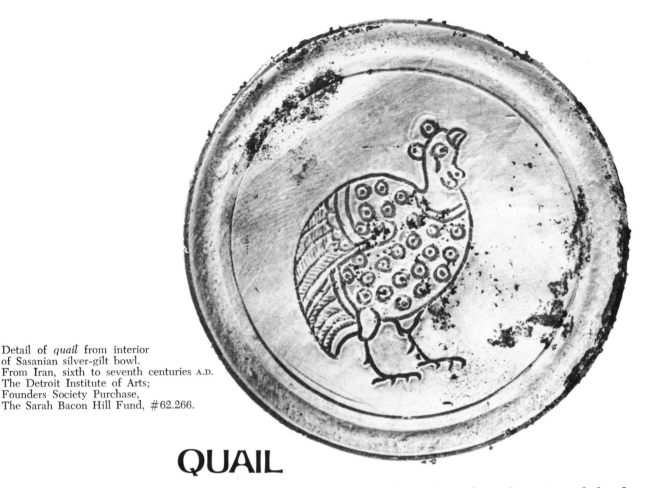

Detail of *quail* from interior
of Sasanian silver-gilt bowl.
From Iran, sixth to seventh centuries A.D.
The Detroit Institute of Arts;
Founders Society Purchase,
The Sarah Bacon Hill Fund, #62.266.

QUAIL

HUDDLED ON THE GROUND in a tight circle, tails spoking inward, heads pointing outward, a covey of quail crowds together to keep warm during the night. The formation also gives the roosting flock safety in numbers should an enemy startle their cluster into a burst of flight, like feathered shrapnel.

The Bobwhite (*Colinus virginianus*) is one of thirty-three species of quails in the New World. Despite its short wing span on a stubby 10-inch body, it flies fast and straight. Its ruddy feathers are speckled with buff and black. This non-migratory bird befriends the farmer by eating weed seeds and harmful insects while its bolder brother dwelling in a city park entertains urban folks by singing "Bobwhite!" from the treetops. This is the name the bird always insists upon calling himself, even though people in our southern states prefer the title of "partridge." (Ornithologists do classify the New World quail in the same family as the Old World Partridge (*Perdix perdix*) which was introduced into our northern states in the late 1800s.)

The California Quail (*Lophortyx californicus*) of western lowlands is about an inch longer than the eastern bobwhite. Both sexes are helmeted with a glossy black crown that tapers into a forward-curving black plume.

The Common Quail (*Coturnix coturnix*) of Europe, Asia, and Africa is about 7 inches in length. Its blunt, brownish body appears incapable of long flight, but despite its improbable contour the bird migrates thousands of miles each year between its northern nesting ground and its southern winter playground. Quails nest on the ground and are prolific egg-layers.

Quails have always been favorite gamebirds of sportsmen. C. W. Dickey has written that when Dixie is played in the South, a gentleman stands at attention and holds his right hand over his heart, and that he shows equal reverence when bobwhite quail hunting is even casually mentioned.

Because body fat is lacking, quail meat should be well larded and basted. Many quails are raised on game farms for the commercial market.

QUAILS, GRAPED ALL AROUND

4 Bobwhite quails, split down the back

4 tablespoons butter

1 cup white grapes, (peeled, seeded, or halved, depending on variety)

12 juniper berries

Blot birds dry, inside and outside, with towel. Sauté birds in butter until browned. Stuff each bird with ¼ cup grapes and 3 juniper berries.

About 16 large fresh grape leaves

4 tablespoons dry sherry

Place a leaf in large bowl, cover leaf with boiling water, add another leaf, pour in more boiling water, and keep repeating until all leaves are wilted. Wrap each bird in 4 leaves so it is thoroughly encased. Place birds in baking dish. Pour remaining butter over birds. Pour a tablespoon of wine over each bird. Cover dish tightly. Bake in preheated 350°F oven for 1 hour.

4 large slices white bread

Toast each slice of bread, trim away its crusts, and cut into 2 triangles.

2 teaspoons arrowroot

2 tablespoons dry sherry

¼ teaspoon salt

⅛ teaspoon white pepper

Remove birds from baking dish. Combine arrowroot, sherry, salt, and pepper, and add to juices in baking dish. Over low heat, stir until smoothly thickened, but do not boil. Unwrap birds and discard leaves. On individual preheated plates, serve each bird on 2 triangles of toast, basted with hot sauce. Serves 4.

PHEASANT

PSYCHEDELIC COLORS are rampant on all male pheasants. Difficult to judge, however, is which of the fifty splendorous species has the most riotous colors of all. Or the most pugnacious voice!

The Common Ringnecked Pheasant (*Phasianus colchicus*), measuring 36 inches in length, half of which is tail, originated long ago in Colchi, an ancient province east of the Black Sea. In time travellers carried the spectacular bird to England and China and many other lands, the son-in-law of Benjamin Franklin being one of the first to introduce it into this country. The hardy ringneck, which is perhaps America's most popular game bird today, is a mixture of many of the forty races developed from the original species. Its iridescent emerald neck and copper body are accented with azure, ruby, gold, and black—which seem contribution enough to the pleasures of the world. Beneath the rainbow plumage, however, lies a white-meated breast, long the target of those who feast on more than hue.

Despite the hungry hunter, the pheasant flourishes, perhaps much like the bird it is said to truly be: the fabled Phoenix that lived five hundred years, then cremated itself on a nest, only to be reborn again as a resplendent likeness rose from the ashes, affirming the regeneration of body and spirit for another five hundred years.

PHEASANT LIVER PÂTÉ

½ pound pheasant livers

6 tablespoons butter

1 tablespoon cognac

Cut each liver into four sections. Discard any tough membranes. Melt butter in small saucepan. Add livers and cognac, bring just to boiling point, and simmer for 6 minutes, stirring frequently.

1 tablespoon minced shallots

1 tablespoon chopped fresh chives, or 1 teaspoon dried chives

¼ teaspoon salt

¼ teaspoon powdered ginger

⅛ teaspoon ground cloves

⅛ teaspoon ground white pepper

Pour contents of saucepan into food blender (or else chop liver very, very finely on cutting board). Add shallots, chives, salt, ginger, cloves, and pepper. Blend well. Chill thoroughly. Serve as an appetizer spread with tablewater crackers or rye rounds. Yield: about 1¼ cups.

Royal Vienna porcelain platter with painting of a *pheasant*.
Early twentieth century. Length 18 inches.
Courtesy of San Antonio Museum Association, Witte Memorial Museum, San Antonio.

Yoruba wooden dish, with cover,
in the form of a *chicken.*
From Nigeria.
Height 16 centimeters, length 32 centimeters.
Private collection C. P. Meulendijk, Rotterdam, Netherlands.

CHICKEN

THE ANCESTOR OF ALL CHICKENS is the pheasant. About six thousand years ago man began to tame the Red Jungle Fowl (*Gallus gallus*), the pheasant from whom all of today's domestic chickens are descended. This chromatic fowl, 30 inches long, still lives wild in wooded mountains of southeastern Asia. In the course of many centuries, however, poultrymen in other parts of the world have bred more than 170 varieties of *Gallus gallus*, some for ornamental beauty or fighting, others for meat and eggs.

A fowl has a comb on its small head, wattles beneath its short down-curved beak, blunt wings bending around a thick body, and a long arched tail. It flies well for short distances with a burst of wing-beats followed by a slow glide, and it runs well on sturdy naked legs, but it cannot swim. It scratches the ground for seeds and insects with three front toes and perches on branches with the counterbalance of an elevated hind toe; the male, called a cock, has spurs for fighting. The fowl spends most of its time on the ground; few species migrate. The polygamous male devotes much time to his public image, while the dowdy female builds a nest on the ground, lays eggs, and attends the chores of raising a brood of chicks.

The white or barred Plymouth Rocks and the red New Hampshire are the leading chicken breeds in the United States today. The Rock Cornish hen is a small hybrid usually marketed at the age of 6 weeks when it weighs about 1¼ pounds and supplies meat for one person. Chickens sold as broilers and fryers are from 6 to 13 weeks old and weigh up to 4 pounds. Roasters are 4 to 6 months old and weigh under 5 pounds. Stewing chickens are anything beyond that age. Capons are male chickens whose reproductive organs have been removed to increase their production of meat and who weigh 4 or more pounds.

64

CHICKEN PIQUANT, WITH WHOLE WHEAT NOODLES

1 tablespoon lemon juice

1 tablespoon olive oil

½ teaspoon coriander

¼ teaspoon thyme

¼ teaspoon salt

1 clove garlic, crushed

One 2½-pound chicken

In medium-sized bowl, combine lemon juice, olive oil, coriander, thyme, salt, and garlic. Remove uncooked meat from bones and skin; mix meat with contents of bowl. Marinate while preparing noodles and sauce, rotating meat once during that interval.

1 small white onion, peeled

½ teaspoon salt

¼ teaspoon whole peppercorns

In kettle, cover chicken bones with water. Add onion, salt, and peppercorns. Bring to boil and simmer for ½ hour. Strain stock and reduce to 1¼ cups, without fat.

3 quarts water

1 teaspoon salt

1 tablespoon olive oil

5 ounces whole wheat noodles

Bring water, salt, and olive oil to rolling boil in large kettle. Scatter noodles into water and cook until barely tender. Drain. Transfer noodles to oiled casserole (about 6"x10"x2").

2 tablespoons butter

2½ tablespoons flour

2 large egg yolks

¼ cup dry vermouth

Melt butter in top of double boiler placed over simmering water. With wire whisk, stir in flour and cook for 5 minutes. Add 1¼ cups de-fatted chicken stock and continue cooking for 20 minutes, stirring occasionally. With fork, beat egg yolks with vermouth; stir into chicken sauce and cook for 5 minutes, stirring frequently.

1 tablespoon olive oil

1 tablespoon butter

Generous pinch of saffron fibers

Over low heat, combine olive oil and butter in skillet. With scissors, cut saffron fibers into tiny pieces and add to skillet. Discard garlic. Sauté meat in oils only until pink colors disappear from meat surfaces. Pour pan drippings over noodles and mix lightly. Distribute chicken over noodles. Distribute egg sauce over chicken. Cover tightly. Bake in preheated 325°F oven for exactly 30 minutes. Serves 4 or 5.

PEACOCK

THE SHRILL, UNEARTHLY SCREECH of the peacock is not in keeping with the regal train he majestically parades before his harem. It is said his rasping voice is ever harsh because each time he looks down at his ugly feet he laments, "Would they but match my feathers!"

The Blue Peafowl (*Pavo cristatus*) originated in and still lives wild in the open forests of India and Sri Lanka. Since Solomon's time, the ornamental male, or peacock, has been tamed as a showpiece in royal gardens and zoos around the world. He is a close relative of the pheasant and may grow to a length of 7 feet, four-fifths of which is a long green train of spotted coverts that cascade over his true tail feathers. At will he can erect this magnificent train into a hundred-eyed fan braced aloft by brown tail quills from behind. His barbed crest, burnished green head, and lustrous blue neck and breast contrast with his chestnut wings and tail. If required to live with other farmyard animals, the haughty peacock is apt to be a wrangling neighbor. The female, or peahen, is without train or noteworthy color.

The Roman orator Quintus Hortensius (114–50 B.C.), in keeping with the ostentations of his time, set off a long cycle of gastronomic fashion when he introduced the banquet dish of roasted peacock. For a while thereafter no feast was competitively complete without a sumptuous service of exotic peacock, but in time the meat fell from favor as it acquired a reputation for toughness and indigestibility. By some accounts the flesh was so tough as never to mortify, although that quality no doubt can be attributed more to a heavy dosage of cooking spices than to mystical powers of longevity.

In the Middle Ages the bird again became popular, this time as the leading dish in a procession of foods heralded into a banquet hall. The bird's preparation was elaborate: it was carefully skinned; its feet were removed; its head was wrapped in linens which were kept wet to protect the crown while the rest of the bird was roasted on a spit; the cooked bird was encased in its original feathers with its train fully spread; its head and feet were gilded and properly positioned; and camphor-soaked cotton was stuffed into the beak and set aflame as the bird was brought before the guests. The bird was usually carried on a golden platter by the party's most beautiful or most distinguished lady to the master of the household or to the most celebrated nobleman present who in turn had the responsibility of carving the bird with his sword so that each diner received an equitable share. Exalting oaths were sworn to the peacock as an important part of the eulogistic affair.

Experienced culinary writers of today suggest that only a young peahen is worth preparing for the table.

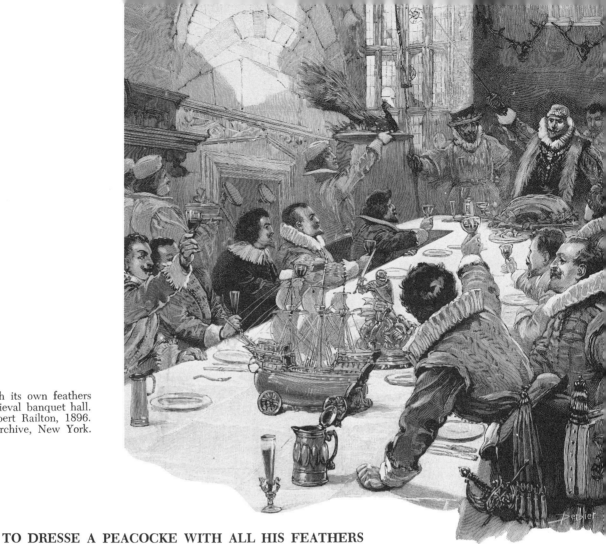

Roasted *peacock* decorated with its own feathers
and paraded into medieval banquet hall.
Drawn by Paul Hardy and Herbert Railton, 1896.
The Bettmann Archive, New York.

TO DRESSE A PEACOCKE WITH ALL HIS FEATHERS

(from Giovanni de' Rosselli's EPULARIO, OR, THE ITALIAN BANQUET,
a translation from Italian into English. London, 1598.)

"To dresse a Peacocke with all his feathers, in such sort that when it is enough
it shall seem to bee alive and call fire out of the mouth. You must kill the Peacocke with a feather or quill pricked into her head, or else make her bleed under
the throat like a kid, then clean the skin under the breast, that is from the neck
unto the taile, and flea it off, and being fleaed turn the skin of the neck outward
neere to his head, and cut the necke, so that his head be fast to the skin, and
like wise let his legges hang to the skin, then stuffe it full of some dainty pudding, with spices, and take whole cloves, and stick them in his breast, and to spit
him and rost him by a soft fire, and about his neck wrap a wet cloth, that the
fire may not frie it overmuch, still setting the cloth: and when it is rosted, take
it off the spit, and put it into the skinne, then you must have a certain hook
cunningly made fast to a trencher, which shall go through the Peacockes feet
and not bee seene, that so the Peacocke may stand upon his feet, with his head
upright, as tho hee were alive, and dresse his tail in such manner, that it may be
round. If you will have the Peacocke cast fire at the mouth, take an ounce of
Camphora wrapped about with cotton, and put it in the Peacockes bill with a
little Aquanity, or very strong wine, and when you will send it to the table, set
fire to the Cotton, and hee will cast fire a good while after. And to make the
greater shew, when the Peacocke is rosted, you may gild it with leafe gold, and
put the skin upon the said gold, which may be spiced very sweet. The like may
be done with a Fessant, or other birds."

67

Black-figured ceramic skyphos depicting a *guinea fowl*.
From Greece, sixth century B.C.
Height 4¼ inches, width 8¼ inches.
The Metropolitan Museum of Art, New York;
Rogers Fund, #41.162.125.

GUINEA FOWL

WATCHDOG OF THE FARMYARD is the wary Helmeted Guinea Fowl (*Numida meleagris*) who cackles a harsh alarm at the slightest hint of intruders. His flock then runs, rather than flies, from the approaching threat, although the birds can fly very well if they wish—which isn't often. Each evening they do wing into trees to roost, their strident cries rising and fading in a raucous chorus as they slowly settle down for the night. Unlike the contrasting garb of the sexes in the pheasant and the peacock, to whom the guinea fowl is related, the male and female guinea fowl wear much the same-colored raiment. Sleek gray feathers with white polka dots cover a bulbous body that tapers into an insignificant tail, the bird's overall length being about 22 inches. A naked head is topped with a bony helmet and hung with a red wattle.

The guinea fowl originated in the bushy grasslands and open forests of Africa and Madagascar. In ancient times it was carried to Greece and Rome where it became known as the Numidian Hen, but the bird seemingly disappeared during the early Christian era. It was reintroduced to Europe in the fifteenth century by Portuguese sailors plying the coast of Guinea and has since been domesticated in most parts of the world.

The flesh of guinea fowl is likened to pheasant, both in flavor and in manner of preparation for the table. Because the guinea fowl is not as profitable nor as easy to raise as a chicken, it is usually produced by poultrymen today only for the gourmet market.

68

GUINEA FOWL WITH FIGS AND PINE NUTS

6 dried figs

Juice of 1 lime

¾ cup sweet vermouth

Combine figs, lime juice, and vermouth in small bowl.

1 leek, minced

1 tablespoon butter

⅓ cup pine nuts (pignolas)

¼ teaspoon salt

⅛ teaspoon ground white pepper

1 cup cooked white rice

Over low heat, sauté leek in butter until slightly translucent. Add pine nuts, salt, pepper, and rice. (For directions on rice, see page 3.)

2¼-pound guinea fowl split lengthwise in half

2 large rectangles aluminum foil

2 tablespoons melted butter

Stuff cavity of each half-bird with rice/nut mixture. Place rectangle of foil over each stuffed top and invert bird onto baking dish; bend foil upward and tear off foil corners to make 2-inch fence around each bird. Brush skins with butter. Add figs and their marinade to baking dish. Cover. Roast in preheated 325°F oven for 1½ hours, basting birds occasionally. Remove cover and roast for 30 more minutes for final browning.

4 tablespoons apricot brandy

Remove birds from oven. Transfer birds, foil side down, to preheated individual plates; slip foil away from birds. Heat brandy slightly in small metal cup. Pour over birds and ignite with match. Ladle juices over birds until flames expire. Serve birds garnished with figs. Serves 2.

TURKEY

THE NATIONAL EMBLEM OF THE UNITED STATES would have been the lordly wild turkey and not the predatory, carrion-eating bald eagle if the wish of Benjamin Franklin had come true. The Common Turkey (*Meleagris gallopavo*) is descended from species that evolved in North America about forty million years ago. The Aztecs were domesticating a variety with a white-tipped tail and black legs when the European explorers arrived in Mexico, and Conquistadores carried prize turkeys along with glittering gold when they returned to Spain early in the sixteenth century. The turkeys soon became popular in many parts of the Old World, and the Pilgrims in turn brought offspring of the original Mexican stock back to the New World in 1620. It is the northern wild variety of *M. gallopavo* with bronze-tipped tail and pink legs that became famous for its part in the first Thanksgiving feast. As colonists and settlers pushed into the open woodlands that fostered the wild turkey, the range of the bird receded into the southern United States and Mexico. The last wild turkey of that era was seen in New England in the winter of 1850/1851. Within the past few decades, however, prudent game management and habitat improvement have revived the bird so that restricted hunting is now permitted in thirty-four of our states.

Like its relatives the pheasant and other fowls, the non-migratory turkey spends most of its time foraging for food on the forest floor, flying ably if necessary, and roosting in trees at night. The plumage of the male, or tom, is as radiant as autumn leaves and seems far more the object of his affection than do the sombre hens who build the nests and raise the poults. A corunculated scarlet wattle hangs from the tom's bare, blue head and puffs over his tufted chest when he arcs his tail feathers and struts and gobbles to his harem. The wild male may grow to a length of 4 feet and weigh over 22 pounds. Many domestic varieties have larger, fleshier bodies with shorter legs and necks. The Bronze, Holland White, and Bourbon Red are three popular breeds. The Beltsville turkey, weighing 4 to 9 pounds, was bred in Maryland for small ovens.

Faience tureen in the form of a *turkey*.
From Strasbourg, France, about 1755.
Musée de Cluny, #7.417; photo, Musées Nationaux, Paris.

TURKEY BREAST STUFFED WITH PECANS AND BOURBON

1 uncooked turkey breast, boned and skinned; about 3 pounds net

Slice each half-breast lengthwise into 4 pieces as flat and as equal as possible. Remove undesirable sinew and membranes. Pound each piece with mallet until meat is ¼ inch thick, or less. Be careful not to split the flesh.

¾ cup shelled pecans, broken into small pieces

½ cup fresh mushrooms, minced

¾ cup dry bread crumbs

½ cup leeks, minced

1 tablespoon fresh chives, minced

¼ cup bourbon

¼ cup butter, melted

½ teaspoon salt

⅛ teaspoon white pepper

½ teaspoon powdered meat tenderizer

Combine pecans, mushrooms, bread crumbs, leeks, chives, bourbon, butter, salt, and pepper. Spread flat the 8 pieces of turkey meat. Sprinkle each piece with tenderizer. Spoon ⅛ of the stuffing onto the center of each piece. Fold the edges of the meat around and over the stuffing to form a somewhat flat envelope.

6 tablespoons flour

1 teaspoon salt

⅛ teaspoon white pepper

2 large eggs

½ cup pecans, pulverized (sold as "pecan meal")

½ cup dry bread crumbs

Combine flour, salt, and pepper on a pie plate. Beat eggs in medium-sized bowl. Combine pecans and crumbs on another pie plate. Gently dredge each envelope in the flour mixture; dip each envelope in egg; coat each envelope with the pecan mixture. Press each envelope firmly to form a secure packet.

6 tablespoons butter

6 tablespoons safflower oil

Combine butter and oil in heavy skillet. Over moderate heat, sauté each envelope on both sides until lightly browned. Place skillet in preheated 400°F oven for 15 minutes. Do not overbake and thereby toughen the meat.

DOVE

FAITHFUL TO HIS WIFE and attentive to his children, the male Mourning Dove (*Zenaidura macroura*) is the quintessence of a family man. He even gives equal rights to his lady in the matter of dress and size, the female being only a trace duller in color and slightly shorter than her 12-inch mate. Their thick, loosely-anchored feathers reflect the shades of dawn: slate blue and olive brown with blushes of ashy rose and shimmering gold, and here and there a shaft of white mottled with gray shadow. They have small heads, short necks, rather stout bodies, pointed wings and tails, and red feet. Their short beaks are slightly bulbous at the tip to accommodate the seeds and berries that make up most of their diet. Unlike any other birds except the sandgrouse, doves drink water by immersing their bills up to their nostrils and sucking in a continuous draught, not by tipping their heads upward with each sip.

To set up housekeeping the male selects a crotch in a windbreak of trees or on the edge of a clearing and carries twigs to the female who in turn twines the sticks into an artless platform suggestive of a nest. On this informal brushheap they take turns warming her two eggs, and later they join in delivering food to their hatchlings. Naked, newborn birds place their beaks in the mouths of their parents to drink "pigeon's milk," a curd passed up from the adult's crop. A pair of doves raises several broods a year.

Mourning doves thrive throughout temperate North America, some migrating out of colder regions during the winter and others residing more or less permanently in warm areas. Most northern states protect the dove as a song or migratory bird, but in the south the ever-present dove is hunted as a legal game bird. It voices a low *coo-ah, coo, coo, coo,* interpreted as heartbreakingly sad or lovingly devoted, depending on the mood of the listener. The mourning dove is smaller but otherwise quite similar in appearance to the now-extinct Passenger Pigeon.

Doves and pigeons are one and the same, there being nearly three hundred species in the family. Their names are properly interchangeable, although "dove" is commonly applied to smaller members with long, pointed tails and "pigeon" to larger members with short, square tails. The cliff-nesting Rock Dove or Pigeon (*Columba livia*), familiar sentinel of the city square, is the common ancestor of all domestic pigeons. Pigeons are raised throughout the world for racing, for show, or for meat.

A squab is a plump young pigeon about four weeks old just ready to leave the nest. Squabs raised by poultrymen usually are marketed at 12 ounces. The meat is dark.

DOVES WITH OLIVES, BISCUITS, AND GRAVY

¼ cup butter

¼ cup lard

¼ cup boiling water

1 tablespoon lemon juice

1 large egg yolk

Biscuits: Warm a large mixing bowl in hot oven. Cut butter and lard into small cubes and drop loosely into warmed bowl. Add boiling water; stir and mash with fork until mixture is quite smooth. Add lemon juice and unbeaten egg yolk; whip with fork until creamy.

1½ cups all-purpose white flour

1 teaspoon double-acting baking powder

½ teaspoon salt

Combine flour, baking powder, and salt in a sifter; sift into bowl of liquids. Toss with fork until barely blended. Spread dough onto sheet of waxed paper. Place another sheet of waxed paper on top of dough. With rolling pin, flatten dough into a square 9 inches by 9 inches. Place papered dough on small cutting board and chill in freezer for 30 minutes. Place cookie sheet in preheated 350°F oven. Remove top paper from dough and cut dough into 16 squares. Transfer squares from bottom paper to cookie sheet and bake for 30 minutes or until lightly browned.

⅓ cup flour

½ teaspoon salt

¼ teaspoon dried thyme

⅛ teaspoon white pepper

4 plucked squabs, each about ¾ pound

¼ cup clarified butter

Doves: Combine flour, salt, thyme, and pepper in plastic bag. Shake each bird in bag until coated on all sides. Reserve any leftover flour mixture. Over medium heat, sauté birds in butter until nicely browned. Transfer birds to casserole in preheated 350°F oven.

¾ cup chicken stock

½ cup dry white wine

Add leftover flour mixture to contents of skillet. Blend well over low heat. Combine chicken stock and wine; add to skillet and stir until smooth. Pour gravy over birds in casserole. Cover tightly. Bake for 1 hour 15 minutes, or until birds are tender. *(continued)*

Faience tureen, with cover, in the form of a *pigeon*.
From Strasbourg, France, about 1750.
Height 9¾ inches, length 13¼ inches.
The Metropolitan Museum of Art, New York, #50.211.101ab;
gift of R. Thornton Wilson, 1950, in memory of Florence Ellsworth Wilson.

1 cup pitted, green ripe olives

Chicken stock

Simmer giblets in chicken stock to cover. When tender, mince giblets and add to gravy just before serving. Also add olives. Serve biscuits with gravy alongside birds garnished with olives. Serves 4.

BLACKBIRD

IN MEDIEVAL TIMES English pastry cooks sometimes arranged to have live birds fly from the pies they served, and upon occasion they even contrived to have live frogs jump out at startled guests. The ultimate surprise, perhaps, occurred at a seventeenth-century dinner honoring King Charles I and his bride, when the famous dwarf of the Duke of Buckingham titillated banqueteers by emerging from a cold pasty brandishing a sword.

One of the favorite "pie birds" was the European Blackbird (*Turdus merula*), a melodious member of the thrush family. In size and form it resembles its close relative the American robin, which measures about 10 inches in length. The male blackbird's ebony plumage is accented with a beak of bright yellow; the female is colored in dull browns. The ancient Romans fattened blackbirds on grapes in special cages. In 1873 Alexandre Dumas recommended that French blackbirds be captured only in late November when the flavor of their juniper berry diet was most incisive.

American blackbirds are members of the icterid family. The Redwinged Blackbird (*Agelaius phoeniceus*), measuring about 9½ inches in length, nests in northern marshes in the springtime and winters in the south in flocks that sometimes number in the millions. A number of contemporary recipe books in this country suggest ways to cook the bird—usually in a compote or a pie.

TO MAKE PIES THAT THE BIRDS MAY BE ALIVE IN THEM, AND FLIE OUT WHEN IT IS CUT UP

(from Giovanni de' Rosselli's EPULARIO, OR, THE ITALIAN BANQUET, *a translation from Italian into English. London, 1598.)*

"Make the coffin of a great Pie or pasty, in the bottome whereof make a hole as big as your fist, or bigger if you will, let the sides of the coffin be some what higher then ordinary Pies, which done, put it full of flower and bake it, and being baked, open the hole in the bottome, and take out the flower. Then having a Pie of the bignesse of the hole in the bottome of the coffin aforesaid, you shal put it into the coffin, withall put into the said coffin round about the aforesaid Pie as many small live birds as the empty coffin will hold, besides the pie aforesaid. And this is to be done at such time as you send the Pie to the table, and set before the guests: where uncovering or cutting up the lid of the great Pie, all the Birds will flie out, which is to delight and pleasure shew to the company. And because they shall not bee altogether mocked, you shall cut open the small Pie, and in this sort tart you may make many others, the like you may do with a Tart."

Design by Walter Crane, *The Song of Sixpence Picture Book,*
John Lane, New York, 1909.

Sing a song of sixpence,
A pocket full of rye;
Four-and-twenty *blackbirds*
Baked in a pie.
When the pie was opened
The birds began to sing;
Wasn't that a dainty dish
To set before the King?

OPOSSUM

MAMMALS BEGAN TO EVOLVE during the reptilian age as hairy, warm-blooded, air-breathing, milk-producing, four-limbed vertebrates with four-chambered hearts. The marsupials, or pouch-bearing animals, were among the first mammals to appear, although few species survive today. The best-known marsupial living in America is the Common Opossum (*Didelphis marsupialis*) which ranges from southern Canada to Argentina. It measures about 3 feet from its naked, rat-like nose to the tip of its long, bare tail and weighs up to 14 pounds. By night it prowls slowly through the woods hunting for food, enjoying almost any bill of fare. If threatened by an attacker it is most apt to hiss and run away but may react with another possum ploy by "playing dead." This cataplectic defense may be an involuntary chemical reaction and not a willful act of deception; scientists are still studying the matter.

The mother opossum carries her children in a pouch outside her midriff. At birth each premature offspring—less than ½ inch long and weighing 7/100 of an ounce—crawls to this pocket incubator for four or five weeks. Then, along with twelve-or-so brothers and sisters, the youngster graduates to the top of her back where it clings for another eight or nine weeks before facing the world alone. The mother has no fancy aspirations for a Home Sweet Home. The father of her brood has deserted the scene, and she is content to raise her family in an abandoned owl nest or an empty armadillo burrow. She furnishes her nursery with leaves and grass hauled in a loop of her tail. She can hang from a tree branch with that tail, too.

The opossum's coarse pelt with white guard hairs has its ups and downs in women's fashions, but "possum and sweet potatoes" is a favorite dish at southern tables year in and year out. Interest in the pork-flavored meat even increases as the opossum population spreads northward. The animal seems under no threat of extinction, however, even though, for example, more than a million have been taken in Texas in some years. The opossum learned the secret of survival when it coexisted with the dinosaur, and its unchanged body design still works. Apparently no credit to its wits, for its brain is very small. More a matter of its two large families per year.

The *Minnesota Conservation Volunteer* once preached that "wasting is sinful whether one wastes opossum meat or dollar bills" and further applied the rule to other small fur-bearing animals such as raccoon, beaver, muskrat, and even skunk.

In preparing an opossum for the kitchen, some people dip the carcass in scalding lye water for a minute and then scrape off the hair with a dull knife—as in preparing suckling pig. The animal is then roasted with its skin intact.

ABOVE: Pottery vessel of the *Opossum God*.
om Monte Alban, Oaxaca, Mexico, about A.D. 200–350.
Height 7 inches.
Courtesy of Nelson Gallery, Atkins Museum,
Kansas City, Missouri, #31–125/143.

RIGHT: Ceramic drinking vessel
in the form of an *opossum* hanging by its tail.
From Colima, Mexico. About A.D. 500.
Height 6½ inches, length 8¾ inches.
Courtesy of Lowell Collins Gallery, Houston.

79

OPOSSUM WITH SWEET POTATO ROLLS

1 whole opossum (including head & tail), 6 pounds after skinning

¼ cup salt

Water

Hang opossum in cool area for 24 hours. Trim off excess fat. Soak overnight in salted water to cover. Rinse with fresh boiling water. Dry.

¼ teaspoon black pepper

1 teaspoon dried sage

8 small white onions, peeled

1 cup water

Rub meat inside and out with pepper and sage. Place onions in cavity. Place in heavy pot, add water, cover, and bake at 350°F for 1½ hours. Remove cover and continue baking and basting until meat is browned and tender. Serve with sweet potato rolls, fresh persimmons, and steamed greens. Serves 8.

3 tablespoons honey

2 tablespoons warm water

1 envelope (¼ ounce) active dry yeast

Sweet Potato Rolls: In large bowl, combine honey and water. Sprinkle in yeast.

1 large egg, lightly beaten

1 teaspoon salt

1 tablespoon melted butter

When yeast is dissolved, add egg, salt, and butter.

1 firmly-packed cup cooked-peeled-&-diced sweet potatoes or yams

2 to 2¼ cups white flour

Another tablespoon melted butter

Add sweet potatoes, mashing and blending with fork. Add flour and knead until smooth. Place in clean, oiled bowl; cover with plastic; let rise in warm, un-drafty area until doubled in bulk—about 2 hours at 75°F. Knead on floured board. Divide into 16 portions and form each portion into oblong roll. Space well apart on oiled baking sheet. Brush with melted butter. Let rise until doubled in bulk—about an hour at 75°F. Bake in preheated 375°F oven until brown—about 35 minutes. Yield: 16 rolls.

Aboriginal bark drawing of a *kangaroo* hunt.
From western Arnhem Land, Australia. Acquired in 1913.
Height 36 centimeters, length 165 centimeters.
Courtesy of National Museum of Victoria, Melbourne.

KANGAROO

AUSTRALIA AND TASMANIA are about the only areas where kangaroos live in the wilds today, and even there the mobs are becoming small and scarce as men, sheep, and rabbits compete for the herds' feeding grounds. The Great Gray Kangaroo (*Macropus giganteus*) browses in open forests, and the Red Kangaroo (*M. rufus*) grazes on inland plains. Each measures as much as 9 feet from the tip of its deer-like muzzle to the end of its long, tapering tail and weighs about 150 pounds. Large ears on its small head are keen of hearing and, along with sharp eyes and sensitive nose, warn of approaching danger. The kangaroo's greatest help in eluding enemies, however, comes from unusually long hind legs that can thrust its body up to eleven yards in one jump at speeds of twenty-five miles an hour. The counterbalancing tail curves upward during each leap. If cornered, the kangaroo defends itself vigorously by balancing on its thick tail while striking with the heavy claw on each hind foot. A male leader is called *boomer.* A female, called *flier,* carries her baby, called *joey,* in a pouch in her abdomen for nine months after it is born, in the manner of marsupials whose offspring are very undeveloped at birth and require a long period of maternal protection. About forty-seven species of kangaroos, including the smaller ones called wallabies and bettongs, exist today.

Kangaroo meat has been compared to wild rabbit and has also been described as more tender than beef and more nourishing than mutton. Although all portions can be eaten, the tail is the most advertised.

KANGAROO: TAIL SOUP

2 pounds of tail (kangaroo or ox) skinned and sectioned *2 tablespoons olive oil* *Boiling water*	Heat oil in heavy-bottomed soup pot. Sauté tails until lightly browned. Cover tails with boiling water.
Double square of gauze *1 large clove garlic* *1 bay leaf* *½ teaspoon celery seed* *½ teaspoon whole peppercorns* *1 whole nutmeg* *1 teaspoon salt*	Place whole garlic, bay leaf, celery seed, peppercorns, and nutmeg on double layer of gauze; tie opposite corners into knots. Add spice packet and salt to pot. Cover and simmer for 3½ hours or until meat all but falls from bones. Remove spice packet and discard. Remove tails to cooling plate. Refrigerate broth; when fat hardens on surface, peel off fat and discard.
¼ cup pearled barley *1 large carrot, diced* *1 large white turnip, diced* *1 large yellow onion, diced*	Combine broth and barley in soup pot, bring to boil, then simmer for ½ hour. Remove meat from bones, chop meat finely, and add to broth. Add carrot, turnip, and onion, and continue simmering for 45 minutes or until barley and vegetables are tender.
½ cup claret *2 tablespoons fresh parsley, finely chopped*	Just before serving, add claret and parsley. Serves 6.

Ceramic vase in the form of a six-banded *armadillo*.
From Colima, Mexico. Current dating A.D. 100–300.
Height 6¼ inches, length 11¾ inches.
Courtesy of The Denver Art Museum, #NW350

ARMADILLO

ALTHOUGH CERTAIN ANCESTORS of the armadillo were as large as rhinoceroses, species of the twentieth century are only 5 inches to 5 feet in length. They live only in the Americas. The only one in the United States is the Nine-banded Armadillo (*Dasypus novemcinctus*); almost half of its 30-inch length is tail, and it weighs about 15 pounds.

The Spanish Conquistadores conferred the name *armadillo*, meaning "little armored one," on this mottled brown mammal. Bony or horny shields protect its shoulders and rump. In between these shells are rows of telescoping or hinged plates that enable the back to arch when necessary for defense or work. The Three-banded Armadillo (*Tolypeutes matacus*) of South America, which is on the world list of rare and endangered wildlife, can roll into a complete ball. The top of this animal's head and the outer sides of its legs also bear protective shields. One suit of armor is all it gets in a lifetime, so the coat does not fully harden until the wearer is mature.

The armadillo is tooled for a defensive rather than an aggressive way of life. It sees and hears poorly and seems to apply its keen sense of smell only to the search for food. Strong digging claws, a long snout, and a sticky tongue enable it to capture scorpions, tarantulas, salamanders, fire ants, and other insects that make up its diet. Because it finds scant food in frozen ground, the armadillo rarely survives very far north of Texas, Louisiana, and Florida. An armadillo maintains several homes in the ground and frequently finds that roaches and beetles take over a tunnel during its absence, thus providing easy dining upon its return. An adult usually lives alone but occasionally entertains half a dozen friends in its den and sometimes forages with a gang of fifty. Despite its short legs, this normally slow shuffler can outrun a man if necessary. The swifter coyotes, peccaries, and bobcats successfully attack its soft stomach or crack its shell with their feet. The armadillo feels safest when burrowed in scrubby thickets, cactus patches, or rocky crevices. In a river the armadillo can indulge its fancy either by walking across the bottom or by swallowing air to inflate its intestine so it can dogpaddle across the surface.

83

An Armadillo Festival is held in Victoria, Texas, every Memorial Day weekend; citizens compete for honors in racing their armored contestants as well as in cooking them. The tender white flesh of this pork-flavored animal is praised by those who know, especially when barbecued. It was sometimes called "Hoover hog" or "poor man's pig" in Texas during the Great Depression.

ARMADILLO GOLDEN

¼ cup olive oil

2 tablespoons achiote (annatto) seeds

Heat oil in very small pan. Add achiote seeds and place over very low heat for 15 minutes. Strain golden liquid into medium-sized mixing bowl. Discard seeds.

½ cup minced ham

½ cup fresh, minced sweet green peppers

¼ cup fresh, minced medium-hot red peppers

½ cup minced yellow onions

1 clove garlic, minced

1 teaspoon marjoram

½ teaspoon salt

¼ teaspoon mace

¼ teaspoon ground black pepper

Combine ham, sweet peppers, hot peppers, onions, garlic, marjoram, salt, mace, and black pepper. Mash as finely as possible or else purée in electric blender. Stir mixture into golden oil in bowl.

3 pounds armadillo meat

About ⅓ cup flour

Cut meat into individual serving portions. Blot each piece with towel; shake each piece in bag containing flour; tap off excess flour. Heat half the golden mixture in wide skillet. Sauté half the meat, coating all sides with golden mixture. Transfer meat to shallow roasting pan. Repeat procedure with remaining meat/flour/golden mixture. Bake uncovered in preheated 325°F oven for about 2 hours or until meat is tender, basting meat a few times. If desired, 5 minutes before serving, place pan under broiler for final browning. Serve with white rice and green peas. Serves 6.

Pre-Columbian calcite vase
in the form of a *rabbit*.
Probably from Island of Sacrificios,
Vera Cruz, Mexico.
Height about 6½ inches.
Peabody Museum, Harvard University,
Cambridge, #C7351.

RABBIT

MORE HUNTERS AIM MORE FIREARMS at rabbits than at any other type of game in North America today. Countless wild animals also prey on the rabbit. Thus it might be expected that rabbitdom is doomed, but nature has providentially designed this mammal to produce large families frequently, and its future seems secure. About an hour after a litter is born, a cottontail mother seeks a father for her next family. In theory, and under ideal conditions, it is possible that a doe and her partner can have thirteen million descendants in three years. Perhaps the rabbit will become master of the world, not extinct.

Scientists once considered rabbits and hares as members of the order of rodents, but now it is agreed that because a rabbit and a hare have two more teeth in their upper jaws than a rodent has and because their lineage is ancient and separate from the rodent's, they should have a special order of their own: the lagomorphs.

Rabbits are frequently called hares, and vice versa. Actually a rabbit is usually born in a burrow under ground, arrives with its eyes sealed shut and without any hair, and is dependent on its mother's milk and nest for a couple of weeks. A hare is born in a form—that is, a depression in the ground hidden by a bush or a clump of grass; its eyes are open and it has a full coat of fur. A few hours after birth it hops about, and within a week it nibbles its own grass. A hare has longer ears and legs than a rabbit. A hare generally runs to escape from its enemies, while a rabbit hides in the best available bush or burrow.

Like all rabbits and hares, America's Eastern Cottontail Rabbit (*Sylvilagus floridanus*) has a cleft upper lip and wriggles its nose to locate food and to sniff the scents of danger. It also thumps the ground with its hind feet if a warning must be signaled to its friends. The cottontail grows to 18 inches in length and 3 pounds in weight. It has a brown coat accented with a white puffy tail. It usually feeds at night, eating bark, herbs, berries, and grains. The cottontail may use a form in a thicket instead of a burrow for its home.

The yellow-eyed jack rabbit of the western deserts and grasslands is actually a hare. It has enormous ears and unusually long hind legs. The White-tailed Jack Rabbit (*Lepus townsendii*) can be 24 inches long and weigh up to 10 pounds; its brownish coat turns white in winter. The smaller Black-tailed Jack Rabbit (*L. californicus*) stays brown all year round.

The Snowshoe Rabbit or Varying Hare (*L. americanus*) is a hare that measures up to 21 inches in length and weighs as much as 4 pounds. As the hours of daylight diminish in the fall, the outer ends of its gray-brown coat turn white; as the days lengthen in the spring, the coat changes back to its dark tones. Its huge, hairy feet do not slip on ice and do not—like the feet of most pursuing enemies—sink into the snow.

The Arctic Hare (*L. arcticus*) lives among the low rocks of the Canadian tundra. It measures 28 inches in length and weighs over 10 pounds. Its fur is entirely white unless the animal is far enough south so the outer tips turn brown in summer. When the arctic hare runs, it lands with all four feet on the ground at the same time.

The Old World Wild Rabbit (*Oryctolagus cuniculus*), averaging 18 inches in length and 5 pounds in weight, runs freely in most of Europe where it has been valued as an important food resource ever since cooking became an art. The symbols and coats of arms of most French restaurants incorporate the rabbit into their seals. Art connoisseurs find many paintings of European kitchens with one or more rabbits hanging near the stove.

Soft-paste porcelain tureen in the form of a *rabbit*, decorated in enamel colors.
From Chelsea, England, about 1755. Length 14¼ inches.
Crown copyright, Victoria & Albert Museum, London; Schreiber Collection I.151.

Rabbits or hares are hunted in all forty-nine of our continental states. A young rabbit is identified by soft ears that are easily torn and by soft, partially-closed paws. The ears of an old rabbit are stiff and rough, and its paws are worn and open.

Our farm-raised domestic rabbit is descended from *O. cuniculus.* Of the sixty-six varieties recognized by the official guide book of the American

Breeders Association, only two are important for commercial food use: the White New Zealand and the Californian. The best rabbits raised for market are fed sweet alfalfa hay and cereal grains—not strong-flavored greens such as cabbage or kale. Between ten and twenty million pounds of domestic rabbit meat are produced annually in this country. About 98% are classified as *tender-young* (fryers), weighing from 2 to 3 pounds when dressed at 8 to 10 weeks. The 2% *mature* (roasters or stewers) weigh 3½ to 6 pounds dressed.

Wild rabbit meat can be sinewy, dark, and gamy in flavor; it is strictly seasonal and is prohibited from sale in most states. Domestic farm-raised meat is tender, fine-grained, juicy, all white, with a slightly nutty flavor; it is an all-season delicacy. Rabbit meat is very high in protein, extremely low in calories (795 per pound), low in cholesterol, and lower in fat content than most other meats. A rabbit's blood is sometimes included in a cooking sauce; coagulation is prevented by the addition of a little vinegar.

RABBIT SESAME

2½-pound rabbit, dressed	Cut rabbit into serving pieces. Combine lemon
3 tablespoons lemon juice	juice and honey in glass loaf dish. Marinate
2 tablespoons honey	meat in lemon/honey for an hour, rotating pieces once or twice.

¼ cup sesame seeds	Combine sesame seeds, flour, tarragon, pepper,
¼ cup white flour	and salt in plastic bag. Drain each piece of meat
½ teaspoon dried tarragon leaves, finely crushed	and shake it in bag.
¼ teaspoon ground white pepper	
½ teaspoon salt	

4 tablespoons butter	In heavy-bottomed casserole, on stovetop, sauté coated meat in butter until golden brown. Pour any leftover marinade into bottom of casserole. Cover and bake in preheated 350°F oven for 45 minutes. Remove cover, continue baking for 20 more minutes or until meat is tender, basting occasionally. Serves 4.

Porcelain tea jug
in the form of a *squirrel*
nibbling at three hazel nuts.
Modeled by J. J. Kaendler.
Meissen, Germany, 1735.
Height 5½ inches, width 5 inches.
The Metropolitan Museum of Art, New York;
gift of Irwin Untermyer, #64.101.199.

SQUIRREL

"ONE WHO SITS in the shade
of his tail" is the translation of the Latin first name
of the American Gray Squirrel (*Sciurus carolinen-
sis*) of the eastern United States. And an important
piece of equipment that tail is! It acts like a trapeze
artist's balancing pole when he walks on a high wire,
steers like a rudder when he swims, warms like a blanket when he curls it
around his feet, shelters like an umbrella in the rain, and gracefully beguiles
a person on a park bench who may have a lunch to share. Almost half a
gray squirrel's length of 18-or-so inches consists of tail, and he weighs as
much as 2 pounds. This active rodent has four large incisor teeth that keep
growing during his entire lifetime and must be constantly worn down by
grinding and gnawing if he is to remain healthy. He nests in forks or hollows of large hardwood trees. In winter he does not hibernate but lives on
nuts stored one by one in individual holes during the autumn. In season he
also enjoys berries and mushrooms and an occasional bird egg or fledgling.
If danger threatens, he dashes to the far side of a tree, out of view.

The American Red Squirrel (*Tamiasciurus hudsonicus*) lives in the ever-
green forests of northern North America. He measures about 12 inches in
length and weighs about half a pound. He nests in cavities of tree trunks.
When threatened, a red squirrel races to a very high, secure tree branch and
noisily chatters or barks disapproval of the disturbance. He stores pine cones
in large ground caches that sometimes hold a bushel or more.

Squirrel meat is one of the most tender and flavorful of our wild meats.
Some sportsmen say they don't care to bother with such a small animal,
but occasionally they offer a friend a few taken in target practice. Raymond
Camp advised what to do in a case like that: "Accept them with thanks, but
don't invite the donor when you serve the squirrel, for the chances are he
will not be so generous in the future."

SQUIRREL STEW

4 squirrels, or about
2 pounds ready-to-cook meat

¼ cup flour

1 teaspoon salt

¼ teaspoon white pepper

Cut each squirrel into sections. Shake each piece in plastic bag containing flour, salt, and pepper. (Unwrap frozen vegetables to thaw for easier distribution later.)

¼ pound (½ cup)
slab bacon, finely diced

2 cups chicken stock

On stovetop, render bacon in 6-quart, thick-bottomed casserole. Remove crisp cubes and reserve. Over medium heat, sauté squirrel meat. Add stock. Bring to boil, cover, and simmer for 1 hour or until meat can be removed easily from bones. With sieve spoon, remove meat to cooling platter.

½ teaspoon salt

¼ teaspoon Tabasco sauce

1 large Bermuda onion,
quartered and sliced

2 cups (10 ounces)
frozen baby lima beans

8 tablespoons dehydrated
potato flakes

2 cups (10 ounces) frozen
zucchini squash, sliced

2 cups (12 ounces) frozen
or vacuum-packed whole-
kernel white sweetcorn

2 cups (15 ounces)
canned salad tomatoes

To casserole juices, add salt and Tabasco. Distribute onions and beans in bottom of casserole. Sprinkle 2 tablespoons potato flakes over beans and onions. Distribute zucchini over top. Sprinkle 2 tablespoons potato flakes over zucchini. Distribute corn over top. Sprinkle 2 tablespoons potato flakes over corn. Remove squirrel meat from bones; discard bones; distribute meat over vegetables. Distribute tomatoes and their juices over top. Press meat and tomatoes down, so they are submerged in liquid. Sprinkle 2 tablespoons potato flakes over liquid. Cover. Bake in preheated 325°F oven for 1 hour. Serve in large soup bowls. Garnish top of individual servings with warmed, crisp bacon cubes. Serves 6.

Beaver bowl carved from curly maple by Kaskaskia Indian of the Illinois River.
Obtained by Judge George Turner in 1795. Length 19 inches.
The University Museum, Philadelphia, # L-83-6.

BEAVER

On religious fast days roasted beaver was a favorite dish of early French
explorers in the New World. The animal's hindquarters were fish, these
voyageurs rationalized, because its rear feet were webbed and because it
spent so much time in water. Actually the beaver is a mammal scientifically
classified today as the world's second largest rodent. The gelatinous meat
of its tail tastes like pork; the moist, dark, fine-textured flesh of its body is
likened to plump turkey; and its liver is compared to that of goose.

Trail-blazing pioneers in America trapped the beaver for its valuable
chestnut underfur, and the pelts became the folding money of the day.
About 1780 four skins bought a blanket and twelve furs paid for a gun. The
glossy, waterproof fur was in great demand for making men's hats until
displaced by the fashionable silk hat in the 1840s. By then so many millions
of pelts had been traded for supplies and fortunes that the beaver was all
but erased from the countryside. Conservationists began working very hard
for strict game laws to control hunting seasons, and naturalists transplanted
beaver families from the few surviving areas to depleted zones. By 1920
the beaver had re-established itself in many parts of the country. Today

Tlingit wooden bowl in the form of a *beaver*.
Collected in Alaska before 1880.
Height 5½ inches, length 13 inches.
Museum of the American Indian, Heye Foundation, New York, #23/8417.

careful studies have proved that in many areas about one-third of the beavers can be trapped each year and still leave a stable population.

The beaver is said to be nature's most industrious animal. As lumberman, architect, and mason all in one, it fells trees by gnawing trunks with the orange incisors in its powerful jaws, it digs canals that foster wild waterfowl, and it builds dams that prevent floods and soil erosion. Unfortunately waters from some of these engineering projects also back into commercial forests, inundate important roadbeds, or swamp valuable farmlands.

The bank-dwelling European Beaver (*Castor fiber*) is found only in Norway and regions of the Elbe and Rhone Rivers today. The lodge-building American Beaver (*C. canadensis*) thrives in Canada and most of the United States. This nocturnal animal has a thickset body with front feet almost as flexible as human hands. Its flat, scaly tail accounts for a third of its total length of about 4 feet. The tail steers the body in water and props it up on land; when smacked hard on the water, it sends a resounding warning to other members of a colony that danger is approaching. The beaver is a vegetarian that feeds mainly on bark, twigs, and leaves of trees such as alder, birch, cottonwood, elm, and oak—or, according to the season, on grass, corn, berries, and lily roots.

A beaver is said to be spectacularly tasty if it has been eating poplar, bitter if it has indulged in willow, and doomed to failure in the kitchen if it has dined on spruce. A hunter traditionally feasts in the forest by impaling the beaver's tail on a green stick and roasting it over hot coals until the skin puffs and can be peeled off easily. George Frederick Ruxton's *In the Old West* recounts that "La Bonte was fain to confess that all his ideas of the superexcellence of buffalo were thrown in the shade by the delicious beaver-tail, the rich meat of which he was compelled to allow was 'great eating,' unsurpassed by . . . other meat of whatever kind he had eaten of before."

A yearling beaver weighs 25 to 30 pounds, dresses out at half that weight, and is the best choice for the table. A three-year-old weighs about 50 pounds and becomes stringier the longer it cooks—according to some experienced cooks, or it requires longer, slower cooking—according to other kitchen professionals. A few oldsters weigh as much as 100 pounds.

BEAVER AND BEANS

1 beaver, 8 pounds dressed

1 tablespoon salt per quart of water

2 tablespoons vinegar

Remove as much surface fat as possible from meat. Cut beaver into several pieces. Soak overnight in cold, salted water. Discard water. Cover again with fresh water, add vinegar, bring to boil, and simmer for ½ hour. Discard water.

¼ cup maple syrup

2 tablespoons dark rum

¼ teaspoon ground black pepper

Place meat in Dutch oven. Pour syrup, rum, and pepper over meat. Bake at 325°F for 3 hours or until meat is easily separated from bones. Discard bones.

2 cups small, dry white pea beans

6 cups cold water

1 teaspoon salt

Wash beans. Soak in water for 2 hours. Add salt, bring to boil, and simmer for 1 hour. Drain, reserving bean water.

8 small white onions, peeled

Add beans and onions to Dutch oven containing boneless meat and juices. Mix gently. Bake in 325°F oven about an hour. Add bean water as necessary. Serves 8.

PORCUPINE

ERRONEOUSLY the early settlers in this country called our porcupine a hedgehog because it reminded them of the prickly beast they knew back in the old country. Actually the two animals are not even distant cousins, and there are no hedgehogs in the New World.

The Common Hedgehog (*Erinaceus europaeus*) lives only in Europe and Asia. It measures about 10 inches from its long nose to its short tail and weighs up to 1½ pounds. It dwells on the ground, sleeps by day in a hollow tree or rock fissure, and hibernates in the winter. The coarse hair on its underparts blends into stiff, barbless, ¾-inch spines on its back. If attacked, it rolls into a ball of spikes to protect its vulnerable nose, stomach, and feet. The hedgehog is an insect-eating mammal that occasionally varies its diet with frogs, mice, birds' eggs, roots, and fruit. It can indulge its fondness for snakes by suddenly biting a crawler and then quickly turning around. If the victim strikes back, it lands painfully on the hedgehog's pincushion arsenal.

The slow-moving porcupine thrives in both the Old and the New Worlds. The name derives from Latin, meaning "spiny or thorny pig." The Canadian Porcupine (*Erethizon dorsatum*) is an herbivorous rodent that spends most of its time in trees and never hibernates. It measures about 3 feet from its sensitive nose to its 6-inch tail and weighs about 25 pounds. Its dark backside fur is interspersed with long, white guard hairs that conceal about 30,000 stiff, barbed spines. If the porcupine flexes its muscles, it can erect these quills but cannot shoot them from its body. It utilizes these weapons by lashing its prickly tail at an enemy, and the slightest contact painfully embeds the fishhook quills into the flesh of the attacker.

The porcupine makes its den in a rocky crevice or hollow log. To keep its four orange incisors worn down, it must gnaw quantities of bark and other greenstuffs. Sometimes a tree is so satisfying to the animal that it remains aloft for weeks at a time, sleeping with its legs hanging down around a limb, and eventually killing the tree by eating away complete bracelets of bark. Such arboreal destruction causes some states to offer bounties for the porcupine. Other states protect the animal on the theory that a man lost in the woods can easily kill the clumsy, slow-moving porcupine by clubbing its nose; he can then roast the animal in its own skin and thus be saved from starvation.

94

Porcupine carved on a fireplace chimney in the Chateau de Blois.
As symbol of Louis XII (1462–1515),
the porcupine signified that the king had no aggressive intentions
but was willing to defend himself when attacked.
Photo, Musée Chateau de Blois, Loir-et-Cher, France.

PORCUPINE POTPOURRI

Leonard Lee Rue III in *Sportsman's Guide to Game Animals* writes that the only person he knows who has eaten porcupine complained that it tasted like turpentine. Bonnie and Ed Peplow in *Round Up Recipes* qualify that the best-tasting porcupines come from a willow or cottonwood when the sap is not running or from some tree that has no pungent sap. George L. and Berthe E. Herter in *How to Get Out of the Rat Race and Live on $10 a Month* maintain that porcupine meat tastes almost like corn-fed pork. John Langton in *Early Days in Upper Canada* testifies that porcupine is a "most delicious dish not unlike suckling pig, but with much more flavour." Sylvia Boorman in *Wild Plums in Brandy* laments the extravagant waste of meat of porcupines killed as nuisances and then abandoned. She attests that the most and best meat of the porcupine is on the hind legs. Martha Eastlake in *Rattlesnake Under Glass* recommends a method of cooking that can also be used for fish or birds: smear the entire un-cleaned animal with a thick coating of stiff clay, place it on hot coals, add more coals on top, and bake—turning occasionally—for 1½ to 2 hours. Some people prefer to skin the animal by first slitting the underside which has no quills. Joseph D. Bates, Jr. in *The Outdoor Cook's Bible* parboils the disjointed meat for half an hour to remove the fat and tenderize the meat; then he dries each piece, rolls it in flour, and fries it in bacon fat. Mark Jensen in *Alaskan Camp Book*, using the legs only, trims away all fat, soaks them in cold salted water for 6 to 10 hours, drains them, rolls them in flour, seasons and browns them in hot fat, and then simmers the meat slowly for 3 hours in a Dutch oven.

The flavor of hedgehog meat has been favorably compared to suckling pig or roasted chicken.

WHALE

Not a fish at all, scientists decided of the whale about three hundred years ago. True, the whale's submarine-shaped body resembles a fish, and it dwells only in the sea, but like its four-legged land ancestors, this marine creature has two forelimbs, called flippers, each of which encases a five-fingered skeleton, and it also has the bony remains of two five-digited hind-limbs uselessly embedded inside its body. The flippers steer the hulk, while broad tail flukes that spread out like small airplane wings flex up and down to propel the giant. Except for a few whiskers a whale has no hair to slow down the glide of its smooth skin. A thick layer of fat, called blubber and located just beneath thin skin, insulates this warm-blooded animal. A whale cow mates with a whale bull in the manner of other mammals and gives birth to a live calf that is nourished by her milk.

A whale breathes air into its lungs and drowns if it cannot surface for a fresh supply at least once an hour. Through one or two blowholes on top of its head, it exhales warm, moist, slightly oily air that condenses into a visible spout as it encounters the cold air on the open sea. One species can be distinguished from another according to the pattern of its geyser: a sperm whale makes a low roundish puff that slants forward; a blue whale, a thick high spire; a finback, a thin tall column; a humpback, a short broad cloud.

Whales divide into two types: (1) the toothed, and (2) the toothless, also called whalebone or baleen.

The black, square-headed 60-foot Sperm Whale (*Physeter catodon*) is an example of the first group, as are Moby Dick and the reputed swallower of Jonah. Their narrow lower jaws have up to thirty peglike teeth that fit into sockets in the upper jaws, and large throats and strong gastric juices enable them to swallow and digest sizeable prey. Squids are their most important source of food.

Rorquals are toothless whales which are prized for their flesh. Instead of teeth, their upper jaws are equipped with long horny bars that are fringed with hair-like bristles and are called whalebone or baleen. A rorqual closes its mouth on a swarm of planktonic animals, forces water out the baleen sieves with its enormous tongue, and swallows the strained sea midgets that remain. Several tons of herring and shrimplike captives thus make their way down a rorqual's small throat during a single meal. It is believed that the vertical folds in a rorqual's white, ridged chest expand when its mouth is full.

The world's largest rorqual (in fact the largest animal that has ever lived) is the mottled Blue Whale (*Balaenoptera musculus*) measuring up to 100 feet in length and weighing as much as 140 tons. Other rorquals are the dark-gray, streamlined 80-foot Finback Whale (*B. physalus*), the bluish-gray 50-foot Sei Whale (*B. borealis*), and the black, thickset, knobby-headed, long-flippered 50-foot Humpback Whale (*Megaptera novaeangliae*).

For a thousand years the whale has been valued in Japan for its meat, at first because the Buddhist religion forbade the eating of four-footed animals, and later because it was more economical as well as more nutritious than beef. A Japanese cookery book published in 1780 contained 120 recipes on the preparation of whale. Today there are specialty restaurants in Tokyo that serve only whale meat.

Because of the limitations of spears and arrows as weapons, only small coastal whales were hunted in early times. In the seventeenth century Japanese fishermen in small boats powered by oars perfected a way of surrounding a whale with nets and dragging it aground; toward the end of such a battle each man had to abandon his craft and swim for his life to the closest shore. Later large sailing ships made possible the capture of much bigger whales in distant oceans. In 1864 the invention of the harpoon gun headed with a delayed explosive and in the 1920s the development of floating factory ships with refrigeration finally tipped the balance of power so much in favor of man that many species of whale are now in danger of extinction. Since 1937 international conventions have tried to monitor all countries in the taking of whale. The blue, finback, and humpback whales are on the world list of rare and endangered wildlife.

Whale meat varies in quality according to the section of the animal from which it is taken. The red meat resembles beef in appearance and flavor; until about 1969 it was marketed in this country in frozen one-pound packages. The muscle under the ventral grooves is made into whale bacon and resembles pork in texture and taste.

GRAMS OF MEAT	TYPE OF MEAT	GRAMS OF PROTEIN	CALORIES
100	whale red meat	23.90	111
100	whale tail meat	41.00	401
100	beef	20.10	133
100	pork	21.40	145
100	tuna	20.90	321

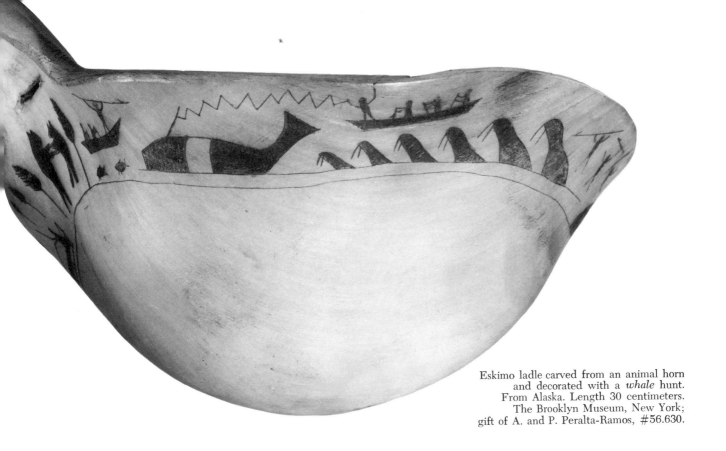

Eskimo ladle carved from an animal horn
and decorated with a *whale* hunt.
From Alaska. Length 30 centimeters.
The Brooklyn Museum, New York;
gift of A. and P. Peralta-Ramos, #56.630.

WHALE WITH MUSHROOMS AND CAULIFLOWER

½ pound fresh whale steak — Slice steak as thinly as possible. Cut each slice into strips ¼ inches by 1¼ inches.

1 tablespoon cornstarch
2 tablespoons Kikkoman soy sauce
1 teaspoon sugar

Combine cornstarch, soy sauce, and sugar in bowl. Marinate steak slices in this mixture while preparing vegetables.

1 tablespoon vegetable oil
½ pound (about 3 cups) thinly-sliced fresh mushrooms
½ pound (about 2½ cups) thinly-sliced raw cauliflower buds
1 tablespoon dry white wine

In thick-bottomed skillet, over high heat, sauté meat in oil for 2 minutes, stirring constantly. Add mushrooms, cauliflower, and wine. Reduce heat, and simmer about 5 minutes, stirring constantly. Cauliflower should be slightly crisp when served. Serve at once with white rice. Serves 2 or 3.

99

射禮おとし心いかにて調た
三尺の木をとめて
熊の首球木のつる
木゛上に上ようも
捲る木をかけ
蚤人かりて
殺し
（胴そ
）

Details from an Ainu hand scroll (makimono):
(1) trapped *bear*
(2) taunting the *bear* with blunted arrows
(3) caged *bear*
(4) drinking sake
(5) *bear* feast
From Japan, about 1840.
Width 26.5 centimeters, length 491 centimeters.
The Brooklyn Museum, New York, #38.648.

BEAR

THE GIANT CAVE BEAR (*Ursus spelaeus*) pictured on cave walls by Paleolithic artists in France is long extinct. The smaller bears that have evolved since that era vary in size and color but have a great many characteristics in common. All bears have massive bodies, shaggy fur, small rounded ears, short legs, and a rudimentary tail. They walk on their heels and soles like a man. Although appearing slow and clumsy, they actually can run swiftly for short distances. All bears have an extremely keen sense of smell, hear reasonably well, and see poorly, although polar bears see better than the others. All bears are loners except at mating time or, in the case of the female, when raising cubs. Most bears are shy or indifferent toward man and do not attack him unless startled, provoked, wounded, or—again in the case of the sow—unless the young are threatened. The bear's savage disposition does not civilize reliably. All bears can climb trees during their cubhood, but the heavier they become, the less they aspire to the heights. An adult black bear occasionally ascends, but a grizzly or a big brown confines

100

その時辟妻の中より
一人おどり出て熊の
両耳をとりてうちのこと
至二人立よりて網と

をしるより何るこ
をわうとそ熊の
あらすべき熊の
旅くるい
山の方なるく
矢球旅はむっく
カモイシンチセンテシウと唱ふ
男麦・小児中でも
矢ところり

ため、岡居する
家の子ケ神初るや
やーアラとて
対るヰ矢ハかぶるの
ところまろる。

矢ハ片羽もあり

its timber activity to clawing the bark of a tree as far as it can stretch while its two rear feet remain on the ground.

All bears can stand erect on their hind feet, giving them much the appearance of a burly, short-legged man. Because a skinned bear has an even closer resemblance to a man, many American Indians felt a special reverence toward the animal and, on occasions of de-robing the bear, offered prayers to help the beast find a preferred spot in the Happy Hunting Ground. Other Indians who believed in reincarnation would not kill a bear because they feared they might be slaying an early kinsman.

The differences in bears are these:

The Black Bear (*Ursus americanus*) ranges in forests from arctic America well into Mexico. Its coat may be black, cinnamon, blue-gray, or even white. It weighs from 200 to 500 pounds, grows to as much as 6 feet in length, stands 2 to 3 feet high at the shoulder, has a straight facial profile, a straight back, and short, curved front claws. In unfriendly territory the black bear hunts mainly at night. In cold regions it sleeps in winter but can be awakened; in warm areas it takes short naps.

The Grizzly Bear (*U. arctos* or *U. horribilis*) lives on the higher slopes of our Rocky Mountains, western Canada, and Alaska. Its coat may be yellowish-, grayish-, reddish-, or blackish-brown, with white tips on the back

イヨマンテヌイヨチマシテ佐倉す〳〵とる

是帽表す一回の大祭事りて
神を祀るより先つ早十年を深山を
兄へ入積雪のすべを熊の嚮ー
さぐ〳〵不をして飼別りたる
を〳〵此して熊と親熊ろ習を
家婦ようさうけて乳味あうて
撫育をや成長すルに
窄へ入て食し鳥肉と
いろ〳〵を喰って冬十月の
あさに熊長大ある
そに日をトして熊と殺さー
酒食とり〳〵
親族用友をまねき
いろ〳〵の若を食せ熊を
食せ神せ
今日チマシテ廿いくまでも
食ー〳〵祝言して大勢の窄を
めぐ〳〵リムセをとる又
撞のめき弓つり〳〵
イナキヲと弓をいー〳〵
窄を入てつり〳〵たき侑
ありー〳〵と喰出そそす
メンコ北さるる〳〵
古例よ〳〵

hairs. It weighs from 350 to 1,000 pounds, stretches from 5 to 8 feet in length, stands 3 to 4 feet high at the shoulder, has a concave facial profile, humped shoulders, and long front claws. The warm half of the year it hunts rapaciously day and night to build up the body fat needed during its long sleep in the cold half of the year.

The Big Brown Bear (*U. arctos* or *U. middendorffi*) lives along the coasts of British Columbia and Alaska, notably in the Kodiak and Kenai regions. Its coat varies from dull yellow to deep brown. It weighs as much as 1,700 pounds, measures up to 10 feet in length, stands 3½ to 4½ feet high at the shoulder, has a concave facial profile and long claws: In winter it sleeps in a cave or hollow.

The European Brown Bear (*U. arctos*) lives in temperate mountains from Spain to Japan, weighs from 450 to 900 pounds, and stretches 5 to 8 feet in length.

The nomadic Polar Bear (*U. maritimus*) swims and prowls all arctic coasts to the southern limits of pack ice. Its fur is white with traces of yellow. It weighs from 600 to 1,600 pounds, grows up to 9 feet in length, stands as high as 5 feet at the shoulder, has a small head with a straight profile and a long neck, and is accented with black eyes and a black nose

pad. Only the female dens up in winter with her cubs; the male hunts
all year 'round, day and night, often in icy water. The polar bear is on the
world list of rare and endangered wildlife.

A bear is capable of delicately nibbling berries from a bush without dis-
turbing the leaves. However, if old bruin comes upon a fawn or marmot
that froze during the hard winter but thawed out long before he discovered
it, he may abandon all gentlemanly etiquette and roll and wallow in the
carrion before devouring it. All bears relish flesh, be it red-fresh or fright-
fully deteriorated, and all bears eat green-growing foods when available.
The black and grizzly bears are primarily vegetarians, seeking nuts, roots,
grasses, honey, fruits, insects, rodents, and small mammals of the woods.
The more northerly big brown bear depends primarily on fish and berries.
The northernmost polar bear must rely on seal, young walrus, stranded
whale, small fish, and seaweed. A bear's weight loss during its winter
seclusion (which is not a true hibernation) is minimal; emaciation develops
after the animal awakens in the early spring and has difficulty finding
enough food to sustain its activities.

Pioneers had a high regard for bear grease. It was a good weather-proofer
for boots exposed to rain and snow, it took the squeak out of a wagon's

103

wooden axles, and it was dandy for keeping one's hair in good condition. More to the point for the kitchen woman, it was considered more digestible than pork fat and was sweet enough to fry doughnuts. Indeed, many a present-day hunter eyes his winter larder with dissatisfaction unless it shelves the clear, rendered fat from a bear. A black bear taken in December can yield from 10 to 15 gallons of oil. One part melted bear fat mixed with one part dark corn syrup or molasses is called "wilderness butter" or "Alaskan butter" and keeps indefinitely.

Eskimo custom dictates that the hunter who first sights a bear gets the hide and his companion who slays the giant gets the meat.

In ancient China and in imperial Russia, the front paws of a young bear were delicacies reserved for the very honourable or the very rich. Prosper Montagne's *Larousse Gastronomique* and Alexandre Dumas' *Dictionary of Cuisine* give impressive accounts of this ursine treat.

Many negativists have had unfortunate experiences with the taste and texture of bear meat. A legion of rapturous positivists, on the other hand, hail the eating of this dark meat as among their finest moments. Age and diet of the animal as well as time of year of the hunt and proper care of the carcass influence all wild game. Because of a trichinosis potential, bear meat should be very thoroughly cooked.

104

BEAR LEG BURGUNDY

1½ cups burgundy

3 tablespoons vinegar

3 tablespoons vegetable oil

1 tablespoon prepared horseradish

1 tablespoon Dijon mustard

1 clove garlic, bruised

1 tablespoon salt

½ teaspoon finely-ground black pepper

For marinade, combine burgundy, vinegar, oil, horseradish, mustard, garlic, salt, and pepper in saucepan. Bring to boil, simmer for 5 minutes, then set aside to cool.

5-pound de-boned bear leg

½ pound chilled salt pork

Tie meat into long cylindrical shape. Cut half the salt pork into narrow strips and lard the meat. Place meat in marinade in covered crock for 3 days, rotating meat a few times. Transfer meat to open roasting pan and pat dry. Slice remaining salt pork into thin sheets; secure sheets to top of roast with skewers or toothpicks. Pour about half the marinade into bottom of pan. Place in preheated 475°F oven for 20 minutes. Reduce heat to 325°F and roast for 3½ hours or until meat thermometer registers 185°F. Baste meat frequently, gradually adding remaining marinade. About 20 minutes before serving, remove salt pork from top of roast for final browning.

¼ cup red currant jelly

Set roast aside on preheated platter in warm place. Ladle excess fat from pan juices. Add jelly to juices and heat; serve in gravy boat. Serve roast with side dish of spaetzle (Swiss dumplings). Serves 10.

105

RACCOON

THE MASKED BANDIT of the woods, the Raccoon (*Procyon lotor*), might at first glance seem a fastidious gentleman to be forgiven for stealing corn from the fields or chickens from the coop. Any robber who scrubs his booty in a running brook before he dines can't be all bad, can he? Alas, first impressions can be misleading, for in truth he doesn't mind if his washing water is muddy or sparkling, and he'll pass up the whole business if the dunking stream isn't close by. At any rate he's enough of a rub-a-dub-dub man to bear the Latin name *lotor*, meaning washer, and the Algonquian Indian name *arakun*, meaning he-who-scratches-with-his-hands.

The raccoon is a relative of the carnivorous bear because of skull and tooth arrangement and because he walks on his heels and has well-digited feet. His dextrous forepaws can out-perform those of any North American animal. He measures up to 36 inches from black nose to tail tip. Black eye patches on a white face form the well-known mask. His stocky body has a coarse, grizzled coat that is frequently sought by furriers, and his bushy white tail with five to ten black rings is a joy to every generation of Davy Crockett hat fans. He swims like an Olympic champion but does not dive below the surface; frogs, trout, and crayfish accessible in the shallows satisfy his cravings. Fruit, fowl, or fur-coated flesh are the targets of his night prowlings. When it comes to living quarters, he prefers hollows in trees to dens on the ground, though he adapts to whatever remains if woodlands are cut down. He is, in fact, so amenable to the shifts of civilization that his families are rapidly increasing. In some areas he is even regarded as a nuisance. Many conservationists believe he should be judiciously harvested so his overcrowded offspring won't be ravaged by hunger and disease. In the South raccoons are active throughout the year. In the North they store up fat in the fall to last through their winter sleeps.

The reddish-brown Coati or Coatimundi (*Nasua narica*) is the raccoon's slender cousin ranging from New Mexico to Argentina. This tree dweller has been called half coon and half monkey. It walks with a long striped tail straight up in the air and slightly curled at the tip. Lizards and insects are its favorite foods.

The raccoon has long been a favorite small-game animal. It gives the hunter and his baying dogs a hearty workout—and satisfying table fare after the chase. A plump young raccoon does not have a full set of teeth and weighs about 4 or 5 pounds; it is usually stuffed and roasted. A middle-aged raccoon has a full set of 40 teeth and weighs perhaps 7 to 15 pounds. An elderly raccoon has worn-down teeth that probably are broken, and it may weigh over 25 pounds. Older animals are usually stewed or braised. Raccoon meat is dark; it is compared to both chicken and lamb, combining textures as well as flavors of the two.

106

Pre-Columbian ceramic vessel in the form of a *coatimundi*
eating an ear of maize. Length 9 inches.
Courtesy of the Art Institute of Chicago, #67.721.

RACCOON STUFFED WITH YAMS, APRICOTS, AND WALNUTS

1 raccoon, 6 or 7 pounds when ready for the pot

2 tablespoons salt

1 tablespoon baking soda

½ teaspoon whole black peppercorns

Remove all fat possible from raccoon. Place raccoon in large kettle. Cover with cold water; add 1 tablespoon salt and the baking soda. Bring to boil; simmer for 20 minutes. Discard water. Again cover raccoon with fresh water; add pepper and 1 tablespoon salt. Bring to boil; simmer for 20 minutes. Remove raccoon. Ladle fat from broth.

2 cups dry bread cubes

1 large boiled yam, peeled and cubed (about 2 cups)

1 cup dried apricots, diced

⅔ cup shelled walnuts, coarsely broken

4 tablespoons brown sugar

1 teaspoon dried savory

1 teaspoon salt

4 tablespoons butter, melted

In large bowl, combine bread cubes, yam, apricots, walnuts, sugar, savory, salt, and butter. Mix lightly. Stuff raccoon cavity with this mixture; sew together the opening. Place raccoon on its side in casserole. Pour 1 cup stock over raccoon. Cover tightly. Roast in preheated 325°F oven, allowing about 40 minutes per pound. Halfway through baking, turn raccoon onto its other side. Meat should almost fall from bones. Place raccoon on preheated platter and keep warm while preparing gravy.

¼ cup flour

¼ cup apple cider or applejack

Ladle off excess fat from casserole drippings. Blend flour and cider; stir into drippings, along with 2 cups of stock. Simmer and stir on stovetop until smoothly thickened. Serve raccoon with stuffing, mashed white potatoes, and gravy. Serves 6 to 8.

Chavín stone mortar in the form of a *mountain lion*,
from highlands of Bolivia or Peru, 850–500 B.C.
Height 6½ inches, length 13 inches.
The University Museum, Philadelphia, #SA4627.

MOUNTAIN LION

THE FELINE FAMILY forms an impressive roster of carnivores. These agile cats all walk on digits which are padded for stealth, and—except for the cheetah—their claws all retract into sheaths, the better to stay sharp when not serving as weapons. They usually do not run in packs but instead craftily hunt alone by leaping suddenly upon their prey. They all have round heads but differ greatly in size, coat pattern, and habitat.

The roaring king of the beasts, the African Lion (*Leo leo*), measures up to 11 feet from nose to tufted tail and weighs as much as 500 pounds. The male wears a shaggy mane over his plain, yellowish coat. He stalks his prey on grassy plains, never climbing trees.

109

Royal titles to the contrary, the fiercest and most powerful cat in the world is the maneless Tiger (*L. tigris*) of Asia. It measures 12 feet from nose to tail tip and weighs 500 pounds. Bold black stripes arc its orange body and untufted tail. A tiger lives in a forest but rarely climbs trees.

The cunning Leopard (*L. pardus*) of the forests of Africa and Asia is admirably camouflaged when lying in a sunlit tree because of black spots or broken rings scattered closely over its buff coat. It stretches 10 feet from nose to tail and weighs up to 200 pounds. The all-black leopards are also called panthers.

The largest and most powerful American cat, the Jaguar (*L. onca*), is 9 feet long and weighs 300 pounds. It has a compact body and a moderately long tail. Small black spots on whitish feet and muzzle enlarge to fractured black rings around central spots on its yellow back. This keen-eyed, tree-loving carnivore lives in swamps and jungles and is more apt to ambush a victim from a tree perch than stalk its target on the ground.

The unspotted tawny Mountain Lion (*Felis concolor*) of the Americas measures 8 feet in length, including its long tail, and weighs about 250 pounds. Its lean body has a small head, long legs, and a loose-flapping belly. It can live in jungles, deserts, or mountains. Although the mountain lion is able to climb trees, it prefers to go after its prey from the ground. Hunters liken its cry to the scream of a terrified woman. Much in dispute is the mountain lion's reputation for attacking human beings and for doing more harm than good in killing wild game. The mountain lion is also called a puma, panther, painter, cougar, catamount, and about three dozen other English names.

The faintly-spotted lynx has tawny fur, a ruff on the neck, tufted ears, and huge padded feet that serve as snowshoes in winter. It measures 3 feet from nose to stubby tail and weighs 30 pounds. It climbs and swims well as it searches for birds, rodents, and rabbits. The Canadian Lynx (*Felis canadensis*) of Canada and the northern United States is closely related to the Bobcat or Wildcat (*F. rufa*) which ranges from southern Canada to southern Mexico.

The Asiatic lion, the jaguar, the cougars of the eastern United States, several varieties of tigers, and all leopards are on the world list of rare and endangered wildlife.

The meat of a young mountain lion has been favorably compared to veal or lamb by many people, including Charles Darwin. Lynx meat is likened to the white meat of chicken. Recipes recommend that tiger or lion be marinated for a long period and then stewed.

Silver cup in the form of a *lion* drinking from a shell.
From Augsburg, Germany, 1677–1685. Height 11¼ inches.
Wadsworth Atheneum, Hartford; J. P. Morgan Collection, #1917.265a-b.

MOUNTAIN LION: GAME MEATBALLS WITH WILDERNESS DUMPLINGS

*2 tablespoons
dehydrated whole eggs
plus 2½ tablespoons water
(or 1 large fresh egg)*

*1 tablespoon dehydrated
minced onions
(or ¼ cup diced fresh onions)*

¼ teaspoon ground cloves

¼ teaspoon salt

⅛ teaspoon ground black pepper

*¼ cup uncooked
whole wheat meal,
such as Wheatena*

*½ pound uncooked,
lean red meat, ground*

In medium-sized bowl, blend dehydrated egg and water. Add onions, cloves, salt, pepper, wheat meal, and meat. Mix well. Form into 20 firmly-packed balls about an inch in diameter.

3 tablespoons margarine

4 tablespoons flour

6 cups water

½ teaspoon curry powder

¼ teaspoon salt

3 chicken bouillon cubes

*¼ cup dehydrated diced
carrots (or 1 large
fresh carrot, sliced)*

Over low heat, melt margarine in 2½-quart (or larger) pot. Add flour; simmer and stir for about 5 minutes. Add water, curry powder, salt, and bouillon cubes, and continue stirring. Bring to boil, gently drop in game balls and carrots, and simmer until balls are cooked through and carrots are tender—about 20 minutes. Remove balls and carrots from broth and set them aside in warm place.

¾ cup dehydrated potato flakes

¼ cup flour

1 teaspoon baking powder

*½ teaspoon dehydrated
minced chives*

⅛ teaspoon salt

*2 tablespoons
dehydrated whole eggs
plus 2½ tablespoons water
(or 1 large fresh egg)*

*2 tablespoons dehydrated milk
plus 4 tablespoons water
(or ⅓ cup fresh milk)*

Mix potato flakes, flour, baking powder, chives, and salt in large bowl. Mix dry eggs and dry milk in small bowl, then add water for eggs and milk, and blend thoroughly. Add liquid ingredients to dry ingredients; blend. Drop 20 teaspoonfuls of batter into simmering broth. Cover. When dumplings are cooked through—in about 15 minutes—return game balls and carrots to broth for reheating. Serve piping hot in wide soup bowls. Serves 4.

AARDVARK

WHEN THE DUTCH settled in South Africa, they gave the name aardvark, meaning earth pig, to the timid creature that rooted the ground like a domestic pig and whose flesh tasted like pork. The Aardvark (*Orycteropus afer*) is a solitary nocturnal mammal that measures up to 6 feet from its long, blunt snout across its arched back to an almost hairless tail, and it weighs as much as 150 pounds. If it swapped ears with a donkey, it would still look the same. Strong, sharp claws enable it to dig for food, or burrow to a home in the ground, or fight a lion, a wart hog, or a python. The aardvark can burrow faster than a gang of men.can dig, and it has stronger pulling power than three men. Although the aardvark eats little else but ants and termites which it catches with a long, sticky tongue, it is not related to the anteater of Central and South America. It has no relatives at all, in fact. Game laws protect the aardvark from meat-hungry Africans in some areas because the animal is so useful in destroying insects.

AARDVARK: GAME SAUSAGE

This recipe works well for pork or beef or most any game, including aardvark. Sometimes pork is combined with game meat. Strong-flavored game may be mellowed by soaking overnight in salted water.

4 pounds lean meat	Cut meat and fat into small chunks. Scatter remaining ingredients over the chunks and mix thoroughly. Put through coarse plate of meat grinder two times. Form meat into patties. Place patties in skillet, half covered with water. Simmer until water disappears and meat browns on both sides. Yield: about 40 patties (each ¼ cup in volume before cooking).
2 pounds fat	
2 tablespoons salt	
2 teaspoons powdered ginger	
2 teaspoons sage	
2 teaspoons sugar	
1 teaspoon black pepper	
¼ teaspoon cayenne pepper	

If freezer is not available, uncooked sausage can be stored in cool place in ceramic jar covered with thick layer of fat.

Pottery vase painted with *aardvarks* and serpents.

114 From Aulad Yahya, near Akhmin, Egypt, about 3200 B.C. Height 12⁹⁄₁₆ inches.
The Brooklyn Museum, New York; Charles Edwin Wilbour Fund. #61.87.

ELEPHANT

AN OLIVE can be removed as deftly from the bottom of a martini glass by an elephant as a one-ton log can be hoisted from the ground to a high platform by that same stevedore. Such versatile performance is possible because of the animal's remarkable 6-foot nose. This elongated, boneless trunk is all muscle, the better for the flexing elephant to carry food to its mouth, lift loads for its master, or shoo insects off its back with a dust bath.

The sway-backed African Elephant (*Loxodonta africana*) stands about 11 feet at its shoulder and weighs over 6 tons. It has a flat forehead and enormous, floppy ears. The tip of its trunk is equipped with two sensitive lips for delicate maneuvers. Its tusks can be 8 feet in length. Some elephants have lived more than 70 years.

The Asian Elephant (*Elephas maximus*) stands about 10 feet at its shoulder and weighs around 4 tons. Its back has a convex arch, its forehead is domed, its triangular ears are one-third the size of the African's, it has only one knobby gripper at the end of its trunk, and its tusks measure up to 6 feet in length.

With a hide that is one inch thick, the elephant is appropriately called a pachyderm, meaning thick-skinned. In spite of this thickness, however, the wrinkled gray hide easily chaps and suffers irritations from insects. Bristly hairs are almost an inch apart, with a few extras on the top of the head and the tuft of the tail. When temperatures soar the elephant lowers its body heat by flapping its huge ears as if they were fans. Although the elephant's brain is relatively small compared to the great size of its head, the animal is very intelligent. Its small eyes do not see very well. An elephant has massive columnar legs. Like the bear, the camel, or the giraffe, it walks by moving its two right feet forward at the same time and then the two left feet forward at the same time. The elastic sole of its 20-inch-wide foot flattens out when the animal steps in mud, then retracts to a slimmer mass as the foot is lifted—a convenient design for a beast that loves the marshes. The African elephant rarely lies down; the Asian frequently does so. When herds migrate, they shuffle single file through forests and savannas. If a bull becomes obstreporous, he is ostracized by the herd as a rogue and is forced to live alone. Elephant grass is favorite forage of a wild elephant. In captivity, a day's food requirement ranges from 300 to 600 pounds of hay and leafy foods. In olden circus days when young boys earned their admission tickets to the big tent by carrying buckets of water to big jumbos, the haul averaged 35 to 50 gallons of water per day per elephant.

The Asian elephant is on the world list of rare and endangered species. Game laws to save the species are not the invention of twentieth-century crusaders, however. In ancient Egypt the elephant population was being severely depleted by men who sought the giant's meat as a delicacy. King

Bronze ceremonial covered vessel of the type *huo*
in the form of an *elephant*
From China, Shang dynasty
(late An-yang, eleventh century B.C.)
Height 6¾ inches, length 8⅜ inches, width 4³⁄₁₆ inches.
Courtesy of the Smithsonian Institution
Freer Gallery of Art, Washington, D.C., #36.6

Ptolemy Philadelphus (308–245 B.C.) therefore forbade his subjects, under penalty of severe laws, to kill an elephant. The prohibition did not last, and the elephant has disappeared from Egypt. It survives mainly in Ethiopia.

Elephants are the only living members of the zoological order *Proboscidea*. Their ancestors from 2,500,000 to 10,000 years ago, the mammoth and the mastodon, are known from cave paintings and fossils. In recent years well-preserved specimens of each have been recovered from ice crevasses in Norway or frozen tundra in Siberia, and a few explorers, scientists, and sled dogs have had the rare experience of feasting on aged steaks.

ELEPHANT'S FOOT BAKED

In TRAVELS FROM THE CAPE OF GOOD HOPE INTO THE INTERIOR PARTS OF AFRICA
*(London: William Lane, 1790), Francois LeVaillant told about
a breakfast of elephant's foot baked by the Hottentots:*

"It exhaled such a savory odour, that I soon tasted and found it to be delicious. I had often heard the feet of Bears commended, but could not conceive that so gross and heavy an animal as the Elephant would afford such delicate food. 'Never,' said I, 'can our modern epicures have such a dainty at their tables; let forced fruits and the contributions of various countries contribute to their luxury, yet cannot they procure so excellent a dish as I have now before me.'"

*Sir Samuel W. Baker, the English explorer in Africa, on more than one
occasion recounted his impressions of elephant meat, particularly the feet.*
In TRUE TALES FOR MY GRANDSONS *(New York: Macmillan, 1884), he wrote:*

"The natives of Ceylon refuse the flesh of the elephant, as do mostly those of India. I have frequently eaten it in Africa, where it is generally esteemed; and although it is inferior to beef or mutton, I have considered it too good to waste. The fat, when boiled down, is useful for cooking purposes, or for making soap, and the foot is excellent if baked for a sufficient time in a slow oven. This is a long operation, as the result will not be satisfactory under thirty-six hours, which necessitates the occupation of the camp for a lengthened period.

"The best oven for this purpose is a hole in the ground, which should be dug with perpendicular sides like a well, about two and a half feet in diameter, and nearly four feet deep. The sides should be well smeared or plastered with tempered clay or mud, rubbed perfectly smooth and allowed to dry. In a hot climate a couple of hours will effect this. A fire should now be lighted at the bottom, and this should be gradually fed until it blazes high above the surface, fresh fuel being constantly added for some hours in substantial logs until the hole shall have become half filled with glowing embers.

"The elephant's foot should be well washed, and then laid with the sole upon the embers while still wet. The mouth of the hole should then be closed in the following manner, as success will depend upon its being effectually stopped.

"Some strong bars of green wood must be laid across close together; upon these, cross-ways, some smaller green-wood sticks should be arranged. This lid should be covered with a few armfuls of wetted green grass, or leaves (should grass be absent), and the mass should be well pressed together. Wetted earth, tempered into the consistency of clay, should be well beaten upon the grass until it becomes thick and solid, after which earth must be shovelled upon the mound and stamped firmly down until it resembles an ordinary grave in a churchyard. If this is carefully watered and well beaten by a spade it will form a covering that will prevent the escape of heat, and after thirty-six hours, when opened, the oven will be found thoroughly hot, while the elephant's foot will be deliciously cooked. The horny sole will detach like a shoe from a human foot, exposing a delicate white surface like a silk stocking. This is thoroughly good eating when hot; and with oil and vinegar when cold; it is far better than the well-known Oxford brawn."

ZEBRA

EXTINCTION IS A REAL THREAT to the dramatically-striped zebra of Africa. The lion was once the zebra's worst enemy, but man now takes a greater toll than the lion. Only three species of zebras remain; two are being maintained safely through management, and the third, the Mountain Zebra (*Equus zebra*), is on the endangered list. The largest, Grevy's Zebra (*E. grevyi*) of Ethiopia and Kenya, stands 5 feet at the withers and has the narrowest as well as the greatest number of black stripes on its whitish coat, long ears, short stiff mane, and tufted tail. When grazing in tall grass, particularly at night when seeking most of its food, these stripes help camouflage the animal. Just as a fingerprint pattern is unique to an individual man, the markings of a zebra's coat are never exactly like those of any other zebra. The zebra is a vigorous fighter and difficult to tame; in ancient Roman circuses it was called a horse-tiger.

The only true wild horse today is the almost-extinct Przewalski Horse (*E. caballus przewalskii*) in Mongolia. Wild horses of the western United States are feral descendants of the Domestic Horse (*E. caballus*) brought to Mexico in 1519 by Hernando Cortes.

Today France has more than a thousand shops called *boucheries hippophagiques*, each bearing the sign of a golden horse's head, that specialize in selling horsemeat. Belgium and Switzerland have restaurants whose specialty is horsemeat. Many Continentals regard horsemeat as tastier, juicier, healthier, and more tender than beef. Price is not the attraction, because in 1973 in France horsemeat cost almost the same as beef. Most Englishmen do not share the same enthusiastic preference.

In the United States the Horse Meat Act of 1919 requires federal inspection of horsemeat if shipped interstate or internationally and if intended for human consumption. The act also requires that a slaughter house used for horses be separate from that used for any other animals and demands that the meat be conspicuously labeled as "horse." United States suppliers are no longer able to meet this country's demands for horsemeat, used mainly for pet foods, so the meat is imported under federal regulation from Canada, Mexico, Argentina, and New Zealand.

During meat-rationing days of World War II, residents of Portland, Oregon, turned for food to the plentiful wild horses in the high country beyond the Cascade Range. Housewives appealed to Mary Cullen, home economist writing for the *Oregon Journal,* for ways to cook it. She advised them to prepare horsemeat in the manner of beef, but because coltmeat is tender but not fat, she recommended that it be treated as veal: larded, wrapped in bacon, or in some way reinforced with oils. The addition of lemon, wine, or vinegar, she suggested, would balance the rather sweet flavor of the meat.

The meat of the zebra is said to be excellent, superior to that of the horse.

118

Prehistoric rock painting of *zebras, horses,* and hunters.
From Mtoko Cave, Southern Rhodesia.
Photo, Frobenius Institute, Frankfurt am Main, Germany.

119

EQUINE STEW

2 pounds lean stew meat

3 large carrots, scraped & cut into ½-inch slices

12 small white onions, peeled

1 cup dry red wine

¼ cup vegetable oil

1 clove garlic, bruised

1 bay leaf

1 teaspoon salt

½ teaspoon dried chervil

¼ teaspoon ground black pepper

Cut meat into 1½- to 3-inch pieces. Combine with carrots, onions, wine, vegetable oil, garlic, bay leaf, salt, chervil, and pepper. Marinate for several hours, rotating ingredients occasionally.

¼ pound (½ cup) salt pork, diced

3 tablespoons flour

In enamel-coated cast-iron casserole, on stove-top, render pork until cubes are crisp and brown. Drain meat and blot each piece with towel. Sauté meat in pork fat until each piece is brown on all sides. Reduce heat. Add carrots and onions; stir and simmer for 5 minutes. Sprinkle flour over meat and vegetables; stir and simmer for 5 minutes. Add marinade to casserole, stir, cover, place in preheated 325°F oven, and bake for 2 hours.

¼ pound (2 cups) small, fresh mushrooms

1 tablespoon butter

½ tablespoon vegetable oil

1 cup (5 ounces) frozen or fresh shelled green peas

Wash and dry mushrooms. In skillet, heat butter and oil until butter stops foaming but does not brown. Add mushrooms. Over high heat, tilt pan back and forth until butter is absorbed into mushrooms and then reappears. Add mushrooms, their juices, and peas to casserole. Stir gently, cover, and bake for 10 minutes. Serve with small, boiled white potatoes. Serves 4 to 6.

HOG

THE WILD BOAR (*Sus scrofa*), from which all domestic pigs had their beginnings, still ranges over continental Europe, northern Africa, and central Asia and has been introduced successfully in the north, south, east, and west in our country. Until the age of six months a young boar's back is marked with about ten white lengthwise stripes which by one year darken to a solid blackish coat of short hair with grizzled bristles. A long snout, a thin and muscular body, and long legs capable of a fast gallop belie this animal's relationship to the plump barnyard pig that does not have to hustle its own food. The boar's tail hangs straight down with a heavy tassle on its tip, again unlike its civilized relative with the coiled spinoff. Long erect ears are always alert to approaching danger, aided by a highly developed sense of smell. The smallness of a boar's eyes reflects their unimportance while hunting and hiding in dense thickets or dark forests or caves. Grunts make up a boar's usual family conversation, but shrill squeals pierce the air when it is angered or alarmed. Two long tusks curving backward out of its lower jaw are its deadliest weapons. The average boar stands about 3 feet high at the shoulder, is 5 feet long and weighs about 350 pounds. Except for the older solitary males, boars usually roam in herds. Late afternoon is their most successful time to forage for nuts, roots, insects, reptiles, bird eggs, rodents, and snakes.

Since earliest times hunting the vicious and fearless wild boar with hounds and spears has been a prestigious sport for kings and nobles. In ancient Rome ostentatious hosts vied with each other in their manner of serving this celebrated beast. Guests at the dinner table of Servillus Rullus were once presented a large roasted boar which was skillfully carved open to reveal a second entire animal, which in turn opened to a third; delicacies diminishing in size continued to be unsheathed until at last a dainty little figpecker terminated the series of strange viands. A Macedonian named Caranus gave each of his twenty wedding guests one entire roasted boar as well as a silver platter on which the guest's slave might bear the memento home.

Because the fiercest and largest boars are the greatest challenge to the huntsman but are the oldest and toughest to eat, only the giant head of the conquered adversary is served as a special treat. The head is singed, scraped, and completely boned. The ears are removed for separate cooking. To the diced tongue and a few fleshy pieces from just under the skin are added a forcemeat of chicken, lean ham, truffles, nuts, and other delectables. The boar skin is then re-shaped around this stuffing, wrapped in a cloth, and simmered for several hours in a jellied stock. When cooled, glazed, and duly appointed with ears, tusks, false eyes, and perhaps a flower over one ear, the prized trophy is served forth, especially as a traditional first course at Christmastime.

121

Seven *boars* painted on the lid of a black-figured Chalcidian krater.
From Vulci, about 530 B.C. Diameter 27.3 centimeters.
Martin von Wagner Museum der Universität, Würzburg, Germany.

This custom may have originated in ancient times as part of a Norse midwinter feast honoring Freyr, the Scandinavian God of Peace and Plenty. In England, King Henry II served a boar's head to his son on the occasion of the young prince's coronation in 1170. The boar's-head celebration became an annual event long ago at Queen's College, Oxford, when a student who was reading Aristotle in the nearby forest of Shotover was attacked by an open-mouthed wild boar. The resourceful scholar jammed the text down the throat of his assailant, choked the brute, and delivered the animal's head to the chief steward who prepared it for Christmas dinner. Ever since the college has commemorated the feat by partaking of mighty boar's head each Yuletide season. A choir accompanies the boar as it is borne to the provost, who presents the orange from the boar's mouth to the solo singer of the year and distributes remaining decorations to guests.

The only wild pig that is native to the Americas is the peccary, also called javelina. The Collared Peccary (*Tayassu tajacu*) lives in thorny thickets and scrubby foothills from the southwestern United States to Paraguay. At birth it has reddish-brown hair with one black stripe down its backbone; at maturity it has grizzled charcoal bristles with a yellowish-white band around its blunt neck. The peccary is like a wild boar in many ways, with a long snout, small long-lashed eyes, pricked ears, straight tail, and omnivorous diet, but it is much smaller than the boar, standing only 22 inches or so at the shoulder and weighing up to 65 pounds. The peccary is reputed to be as ferocious as the wild boar, but actually it warily retreats from danger as fast as it can scramble unless wounded or cornered, in which case it fights pluckily out of sheer necessity. Unlike the boar, the peccary has a ruminant-like stomach, its tusks point straight down, and it has a large scent gland on its arched back. The pungent odor emitted from this gland gives a silent but effective warning to a downwind herd that danger is near. It also helps a sow detect the whereabouts of her offspring whose backs rub the underbrush as they wander. And it explains another name for the animal: musk hog. This gland must be removed as soon as the animal is killed if the flesh is to remain palatable.

About seven thousand years ago man decided that instead of hunting in the woods each time he needed meat, it would be more convenient to feed and shelter the wild pig at home so he could convert it to a roast at will. His idea caught on. Today it is calculated that if one sow bears litters to her fullest capacity and if all her daughters do the same, their progeny will number seven million in ten years. China, Brazil, and the United States are the leading producers of domestic swine. About one-third of the meat consumed in the United States is pork.

A suckling pig up to the age of 8 weeks is called a *piglet*. Once weaned, it becomes a *shote* (or *shoat*). A sexually immature hog, usually under 10 weeks of age, is a *pig*. A *gilt* is an immature female hog that has not farrowed. A *sow* is a mature female hog that has farrowed. A *barrow* is a male hog castrated before it is sexually mature. A *boar* is an uncastrated mature male hog. A *hog* may be a pig, sow, or boar. Collectively, all are *swine*.

Most hogs are marketed between 5½ and 7 months of age, weighing 180 to 240 pounds. A fully-developed sow weighs perhaps 625 pounds; a boar, 825 pounds. Important bacon-type breeds in this country are the white Yorkshire and the red Tamworth. Outstanding meat types are the black-and-white Spotted Poland China, the black Hampshire with a white band around its shoulder and front legs, and breeds such as the Beltsville, Maryland, Minnesota, and Montana.

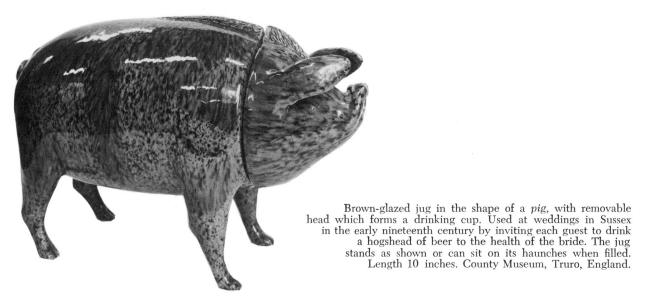

Brown-glazed jug in the shape of a *pig*, with removable head which forms a drinking cup. Used at weddings in Sussex in the early nineteenth century by inviting each guest to drink a hogshead of beer to the health of the bride. The jug stands as shown or can sit on its haunches when filled. Length 10 inches. County Museum, Truro, England.

PORK TENDERLOIN WITH LOTUS ROOTS

24 slices (about ⅜ pound) dried lotus roots

½ teaspoon vinegar

½ teaspoon salt

In saucepan, soak lotus roots for about 6 hours in vinegar and cold water to cover. Drain and rinse. Add salt and fresh water to cover, bring to boil, and simmer for 1 hour.

3 tablespoons Kikkoman soy sauce

2 tablespoons honey

1 teaspoon salt

1 teaspoon minced fresh ginger root

½ teaspoon powdered Chinese five-spices

1 clove garlic, crushed and minced

3 whole pork tenderloins (about 3½ pounds)

In shallow baking dish, combine soy sauce, honey, salt, ginger root, five-spices, and garlic. Marinate meat in this mixture for 1 hour, rotating strips a few times during interval. Place dish in oven so top of meat is about 4 inches under source of heat. Broil under medium heat about 45 minutes, turning frequently for even browning.

1½ tablespoons cornstarch

1 tablespoon rice vinegar

1 tablespoon dry white wine

1 teaspoon powdered Chinese mustard

1 cup hot chicken stock

Combine cornstarch, vinegar, wine, and mustard in top half of double boiler with simmering water in lower half. Add stock; stir until smoothly thickened. Add drained lotus roots and heat thoroughly. Serve pork cut into thin slices, accompanied by lotus roots. Garnish with preserved guava shells stuffed with preserved lychee nuts. Serves 8.

124

CAMEL

ABOUT FOUR MILLION SULLEN BUT USEFUL camels inhabit the world today. About a million are the two-humped Bactrian Camel (*Camelus bactrianus*) of central Asia, and the others are the one-humped Arabian Camel or Dromedary (*C. dromedarius*) of northern Africa and the Near East.

The reddish-brown Bactrian camel measures about 7 feet to the top of its hump and weighs up to 1,500 pounds. It is all-important to many Asian people in arid lands where temperatures, both hot and cold, are extreme, for besides providing transportation, this beast of burden also yields milk, meat, wool, and hide.

The somewhat taller Arabian camel divides into two groups: the baggage camel, which carries up to 500 pounds about 30 miles per day or up to 1,000 pounds for shorter hauls at slower rates, and the dromedary or racing camel, which carries one rider about 100 miles per day. The animal is superbly designed for desert life. Its tan, wooly coat blends with the dunes. Each long leg ends in a broad, undivided pad that prevents it from sinking into the sand. Overhanging eyelids and a double row of long lashes shield its eyes from the fierce sun. Its nostrils close up in a sandstorm. A cleft upper lip is pliant enough to stretch straight out for a thorny plant and yet tough enough to resist wretched abrasions. Strong yellow teeth effectively crunch into almost anything. The hump, a variable lump of fat between the backbone and the skin, provides energy for days without re-fueling. Although a camel drinks about six gallons of water per day by choice, it can go comfortably for three days without re-tanking, and some are said to have survived thirty-four days without taking on water. Need for refreshment depends on the animal's pasture, the nature of its work, and the season of the year. There are scientists who discredit the idea that part of a camel's fat converts to water or that large amounts of water are stored in one of its three stomach chambers.

A camel's disposition is deemed as ugly as its voice, but there are other compensations to its human associates. Its milk—so rich that it curdles in coffee—makes good butter and cheese and also ferments into an alcoholic drink called kumiss. The flesh of young camel is often compared to veal or lamb. Camels were forbidden to the Jews by Moses but were, and still are, common fare for the Arabs. Camel was the favorite meat of Aristotle but was generally disdained by the Romans. In the thirteenth century a Chinese writer extolled the firm hump of a vigorous camel as one of the Eight Delicacies. In recent times on the Sahara desert John Gunther asked if the jeep would ever replace the camel. "No," he was assured, "you cannot eat a jeep if it dies."

Ceramic bowl depicting King Bahram Gour
and his luteplayer Azada on a *dromedary*.
From Persia, about 1200. Diameter 20.7 centimeters.
Collection Haags Gemeentemuseum, The Hague.

In 1919 in *Sudan Notes and Records*, W. R. G. Bond described the proto-
col of herdsmen of Northern Sudan on the matter of camels:

It is improper, he said, for a man to kill a beast merely to indulge his own
private hunger for meat. He slaughters an animal for food only on special occasions such as a birth in the family, a wedding, a visit from an honored guest,
or a holy day. In every case his neighbors are invited to share freely in the
meat.

This is basically, continued Mr. Bond, because an animal provides, as a rule,
too much meat for an individual and his immediate household. Meat decays
rapidly and cannot be stored for future use. Accordingly, if there is to be no
waste, neighbors must be called in whenever an animal is to be killed, and con-
versely, if there is no gathering, there should be no meat. One may imagine that
reputations for hospitality which are so highly valued among the Arabs are more
readily built up by a punctual discharge of this duty of taking one's turn at
providing one's neighbors with meat than by altruistic generosity to casual
strangers.

The consumption of milk or corn represents the spending of income, but the
slaughter of an animal is a draft on capital. From a store of grain, a few hand-
fuls may be withdrawn and the deficit may be made good at harvest time by the
addition of new grain which mingles with the old. A living animal, however, is
indivisible, concluded Mr. Bond. Before the smallest piece of meat can be used,
the whole animal must be dead, and once dead, it is dead forever.

CAMEL WITH EGGPLANT, YOGHURT, AND CHEESE

3 pounds eggplant

2 teaspoons salt

Water

Peel eggplants and cut crosswise into ½-inch slices. Cover with salted water, keeping slices immersed under weighted plate. Soak for 1 hour. Drain; blot on towel.

8 tablespoons margarine

Spread 2 tablespoons margarine over each of 2 large cookie sheets. Distribute eggplant slices on sheets. Bake in preheated 350°F oven for 45 minutes. Turn over each slice. Distribute 2 more tablespoons margarine over each sheet. Bake 30 more minutes.

1 tablespoon olive oil

1 medium-sized yellow onion, finely diced

2 cloves garlic, minced

1 pound lean camel meat, finely diced

¼ teaspoon dried rosemary, crushed

½ teaspoon salt

Over medium heat, sauté onions and garlic in oil for about 5 minutes. Add meat, rosemary, and salt. Sauté and stir until meat is nicely browned.

2 large eggs

1 cup (8 oz.) plain yoghurt

¾ cup (4 oz.) crumbled feta cheese or grated Parmesan cheese

paprika

Beat eggs until frothy. Blend in yoghurt. Add cheese. Distribute half the eggplant in bottom of casserole dish (about 6″x10″x2″). Spread meat over eggplant. Cover with half the yoghurt mixture. Distribute remaining eggplant over yoghurt. Cover with remaining yoghurt. Sprinkle with paprika. Bake uncovered for 1 hour at 325°F. Serves 6.

ELK

EVEN UNDER THE BEST OF CIRCUMSTANCES it might not always be easy for a sultan to keep a harem of twenty to sixty wives contented, but his cause certainly wouldn't be helped by having a constant ring of seductive males nearby, lustily waiting to claim any female willing to tarry. And yet such is the state of affairs for an ambitious bull elk during the season of romance in the high woodlands of the American Rockies. He owes much of his dynastic success to his impressive head of antlers. This headgear—sword, shield, and costume all in one—is shed each winter. In early March a velvety new pair erupts above his brow and by late May grows to a five-foot arch with six or seven tines on each beam. By autumn the antlers are hard and shiny, mighty weapons to wield in fending off bold rivals who covet his cows. This bugling monarch rules supreme throughout the rutting season, then yields leadership to an elderly cow as the herd migrates for the winter from alpine meadows to lower wooded valleys in search of grass and browse.

The American Elk or Wapiti (*Cervus canadensis*) stands as high as 5 feet at the shoulder and measures up to 10 feet in length; he weighs as much as 1,000 pounds. His blocky body is brownish-gray with a black belly, a short whitish tail and rump patch, and with chestnut-brown legs, head, and maned neck. With two hoofs on each strong leg he is able to leap as much as ten feet into the air. His canine teeth which develop into miniature tusks were sought as status symbols by the early American Indians and today are held in special esteem by certain fraternal organizations in this country.

The smaller European Red Deer (*C. elaphus*) is very closely related to the American elk or wapiti and is sometimes considered the same species. Europeans call the male red deer a *stag* and the female a *hind*—in contrast to Americans who call the elk a *bull* or *cow* and the deer a *buck* or *doe*. An American elk is a *moose* to Europeans.

Meat from an elk, called venison, tastes more like beef than does that of any other game animal.

Silver gilt cup in the form of a *stag*.
Perhaps by Christoph Erhard.
Augsburg, Germany, late sixteenth century.
Trustees of the British Museum, London.

ELK STEAK

4 elk steaks,
each 1-inch thick and
each weighing about 1 pound

½ cup melted butter

2 teaspoons anchovy paste

1 tablespoon lemon juice

2 tablespoons
fresh chopped chives
(or 2 teaspoons dried)

¼ teaspoon
finely-ground black pepper

12 1-inch slices
French or Italian bread

Keep steaks at room temperature for 2 hours before cooking. Combine butter, anchovy paste, lemon juice, chives, and pepper. Wipe steaks dry; place on rack which is 4 inches under broiler heat. Place bread on tray under steak rack. Spread half of butter mixture over top surfaces of steaks. Broil steaks for about 7 minutes. Turn steaks over and spread tops with remaining butter mixture. Broil for about 5 minutes. Brush tray drippings onto bread slices; brown the slices close to broiler while arranging steaks on preheated plates. Serves 4.

129

DEER

THE FAMILY TREE OF "TRUE DEER" includes the elk, the moose, and the reindeer as well as the animal Americans call a deer and as well as exotically-named members in more distant parts of the world. Deer are the most plentiful large-game animal in America today. They all walk on enlarged third and fourth toenails called hoofs. All are ruminants with four-chambered stomachs designed to store vegetation until it can be conveniently digested at a later time. They browse on leaves, twigs, pine needles, nuts, fruits, ferns, corn, clover, and cabbage, to name but a portion of their bill of fare.

The White-tailed Deer (*Odocoileus virginianus*) stands a little over 3 feet at the shoulder and weighs up to 400 pounds. It grows two fur coats a year: a red-brown covering of thin hairs in the spring, and a blue-gray protection of insulating, tubular bristles in the fall. When a deer runs, its brown-topped tail stands straight up, causing the white hairs beneath to serve as a signal flag to the spotted fawn or enemy that follows. Only the male has antlers; each long beam has as many as eight unbranched tines. Velvety antlers sprout each spring, harden by fall, and are shed during the winter. The white-tailed deer thrives today in forests and brushlands from southern Canada to South America. About eight million live in the United States, more than one-fourth being in Texas.

The Mule Deer (*O. hemionus*) is about the same height as the white-tailed deer but is stockier and heavier. It is distinguished by mule-like ears and by a solid black or black-tipped tail. Its fur coat is similar to that of the white-tail. The main beam of each antler branches into a fork, and each fork then divides into two points. Over six million mule deer range the sparse timberlands and prairies from Alaska to northern Mexico.

When wolves and mountain lions were the chief predators of deer in this country, sick and elderly animals were usually the victims, and only the virile remained to continue the strain. As settlers gradually killed off the wolves and mountain lions and were joined by sportsmen in selecting the choicest bucks as their trophies, only the weaker deer were left in the woods, and their offspring inherited the worst instead of the best characteristics of the species. In some areas today the survivors are actually tragic. Where harvesting of wild game is not permitted and yet natural foods are inadequate, starvation and disease take heavy tolls, and decimated herds subsist with difficulty and suffering. Prudent harvesting under the direction of professional game managers is frequently considered the best way to retain a healthy, stable deer population today.

Deer meat, called venison, compares to beef but usually requires additional larding or basting.

130

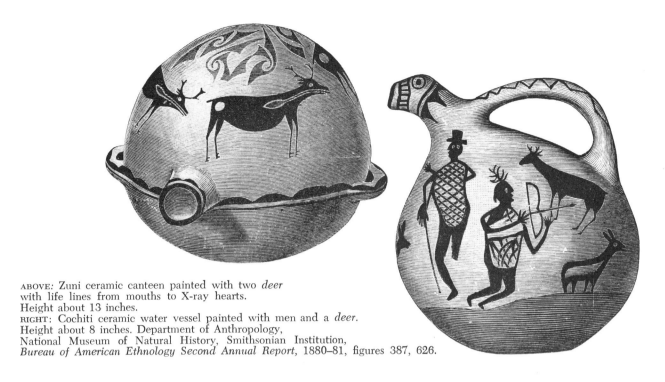

ABOVE: Zuni ceramic canteen painted with two *deer*
with life lines from mouths to X-ray hearts.
Height about 13 inches.
RIGHT: Cochiti ceramic water vessel painted with men and a *deer*.
Height about 8 inches. Department of Anthropology,
National Museum of Natural History, Smithsonian Institution,
Bureau of American Ethnology Second Annual Report, 1880–81, figures 387, 626.

VENISON CHOPS, BREADED

½ clove garlic, finely minced

1 small onion, finely minced

*½ teaspoon
dried parsley leaves*

*¼ teaspoon
powdered mild mustard*

¼ teaspoon salt

⅛ teaspoon ground black pepper

1 extra-large egg

On large plate with high rim, combine garlic, onion, parsley, mustard, salt, pepper, and egg. Beat with fork until smoothly blended.

*4 venison loin chops,
about 1½ pounds*

About ¼ cup flour

*About ½ cup
fine, dry bread crumbs*

6 tablespoons butter

Dredge each chop in flour. Then dip in herb/egg mixture. Then coat with bread crumbs. Melt butter in large, thick-bottomed skillet. Over medium-low heat, sauté each chop about 10 minutes on each side. Serve on pre-heated plates.

1 tablespoon flour

¼ cup water

2 tablespoons port

1 tablespoon lemon juice

Add flour to butter remaining in skillet. Stirring constantly, add water, port, and lemon juice. Ladle sauce over chops. Serve with brown rice. Serves 4.

131

Cut-out pattern of a *moose* used by an Algonquin Indian
for decorating a birchbark container.
Department of Anthropology, National Museum of Natural History,
Smithsonian Institution,
Bureau of American Ethnology Bulletin 128, 1940–41, page 252.

MOOSE

WITH HIS UPPER MUZZLE DROOPING four inches over his chin, a bull moose
doesn't win gold cups for having a classically handsome profile. He does,
however, wear a six-foot crown of flattened antlers that is much prized by
trophy hunters and is greatly respected by man and rival moose alike, for
a bellowing bull moose aroused during rutting season is a fearless assailant
willing to ram his formidable antlers into anything that moves across his
path—even into trucks and bulldozers. These antlers are shed each winter,
then erupt anew each spring as soft, velvety branchings that season into
hard, shiny weapons by fall. Female moose, called cows, do not have
antlers.

The American Moose (*Alces alces*) is the largest deer in the world. A
smaller race of the same species is called an elk in the Old World. The
American moose stands about 7 feet high at the shoulders and weighs up to
1,800 pounds. Its coarse coat is dark brown from its large mulish ears,
across its maned neck, over its humped shoulders, to its short tail; colors
blend into lighter grays under the belly and down its long legs. A whiskered
flap of skin, called a bell, protrudes beneath its throat. Two broad hoofs
and two dewclaws on each foot splay out to leave a track 10 inches long
in soft ground. A moose lives in northern woodlands near marshes and
lakes where it can browse on deciduous twigs and water plants. The bull
does not keep a harem but courts one cow for several days before aban-
doning her for another. Moose do not migrate. They usually live alone, perhaps forming small bands in winter but never massing into large herds.

Just as the bison was once the staff of life for the Plains Indians and the
reindeer was the mainstay of natives of the far north, the moose was all-
important to the people of the forestlands of Canada. The moose is still
vital to those whose location or economy does not permit the purchase of
other meats, and it is held in great favor by those who seek game meats by
preference. The meat is generally a little darker and drier than beef.

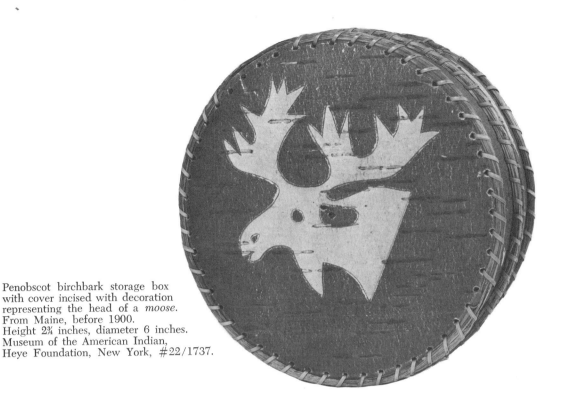

Penobscot birchbark storage box
with cover incised with decoration
representing the head of a *moose*.
From Maine, before 1900.
Height 2¾ inches, diameter 6 inches.
Museum of the American Indian,
Heye Foundation, New York, #22/1737.

MOOSEBURGERS, STUFFED

1 large egg

1 tablespoon angostura bitters

½ teaspoon salt

⅛ teaspoon ground black pepper

1 tablespoon melted butter

½ cup minced celery

1 small white onion, minced

*2 cups very dry
¼-inch bread cubes*

In large bowl, beat together the egg, bitters, salt, and pepper. Stir in butter, celery, and onion. With fork, lightly toss in bread cubes.

*2 pounds very lean
ground moose meat*

6 strips thick-sliced bacon

24 toothpicks

Divide meat into 6 equal portions. Flatten each portion into a "pancake." Center 1/6 of the stuffing on each "pancake." Wrap meat around stuffing. Place stuffed burgers on oiled roasting tray. Cut each bacon strip in half and secure with toothpicks atop burger. Bake in preheated 350°F oven for 30 minutes. Just before serving, place under broiler for final browning. Serves 6.

REINDEER

THE ONLY SUCCESSFULLY DOMESTICATED DEER in the world is the Old World Reindeer (*Rangifer tarandus*). Besides providing the arctic herdsman with meat, milk, and hide, it willingly pulls a sled across the snow. The reindeer's enormous round hoofs keep the animal from sinking into spongy tundra or deep snow. These splayed hoofs with large dewclaws also serve as shovels when the animal claws through snow to reach the moss beneath—whence the French Canadian name of *caribou*, which derives from an Indian word meaning "scratcher" or "pawer."

The New World Caribou (*R. tarandus*) has never conformed to domestication as has its Old World relative the reindeer, although they both share the same scientific name. The woodland caribou is larger and darker than the more northerly Barren Ground caribou; both are larger than the reindeer. A male woodland caribou stands about 4 feet high at the shoulder and weighs up to 400 pounds. Its coat is rich brown in summer and bleaches to gray by late winter. The shaggy hair hanging from its throat is whitish, as are its broad muzzle, short tail, and wide spats. Ankle bones click when it walks. Unlike other deer, both sexes of reindeer and caribou have antlers. These antlers, sometimes five feet long, have sweeping beams with many branches and with at least one brow tine, called a shovel, projecting forward. A males' antlers are usually dropped in early winter, and a female loses hers before fawning time in the spring.

During the last century the migrating caribou of North America faced extinction when vast and repeated tundra fires destroyed their natural feeding grounds and when guns killed them off faster than bows and arrows. Beginning in 1891 reindeer from Siberia were introduced into Alaska and Canada, and the resulting herds supplied many Eskimos and Indians with food. Ecological repercussions have developed, however: not all native hunters accept herding as a way of life; domesticated reindeer readily interbreed with wild caribou, and the feral offspring are unable to cope with life in the wilderness; and at times domesticated reindeer compete with wild caribou for the same grazing grounds. Many untamable caribou are therefore protected today in areas that contain their all-important lichens, shrubs, and grasses.

Many reindeer herds increase each year and yield a surplus of meat even after local needs are satisfied, so excellent frozen meat is sometimes available in more southerly city markets. In 1922 explorer Vilhjalmur Stefansson reported that Eskimos considered the flavor of their venison more important than the tenderness; they therefore fed reindeer hams and tenderloins to their dogs, preferring for themselves the head, tongue, ribs, heart, and shoulder, in that order.

Indians in the eastern woods of Canada and the United States did not need an iron kettle for cooking. They peeled a strip of bark from a birch tree, folded it into a seamless box, and hung it over a fire; if flames did not touch the bark, water in the vessel boiled but the bark did not burn. The contents could also be cooked if hot stones were dropped into the bark "pot." Birchbark containers were also used for storing or carrying food. Decorations were made by scraping away the bark surrounding a desired pattern. The engraved box shown with silhouettes of beavers and *caribou* surrounding a bear was made by a Cree or possibly an Ojibwa Indian. About 1900. Height 6½ inches, length 11½ inches. Courtesy of The Denver Art Museum, #CWc-1.

REINDEER ROAST, CRANBERRIED

Reindeer rump,
4 pounds after de-boning

¼ pound chilled salt pork

2 small onions, sliced

1 teaspoon juniper berries

1 teaspoon salt

⅛ teaspoon ground white pepper

1½ cups cranberry juice nectar

¼ cup gin

¼ cup vegetable oil

Lard rump with salt pork. Place meat in glass or enameled container. Add onions, juniper berries, salt, pepper, cranberry nectar, gin, and oil. Marinate roast for 2 days, rotating occasionally. Place roast and marinade in open pan in preheated 500°F oven for 15 minutes. Reduce heat to 325°F and continue roasting for 2½ more hours or until meat thermometer registers 170°F. Baste meat frequently.

3 tablespoons flour
2 tablespoons butter

Strain pan drippings into saucepan. Ladle off fat. Knead flour into butter; add to saucepan. Heat and stir on stovetop for 10 minutes. Serve thinly-sliced meat basted with hot sauce, along with whole-kernel yellow corn. Serves 8.

PRONGHORN

THE FASTEST-RUNNING GAME ANIMAL IN NORTH AMERICA is the Pronghorn (*Antilocapra americana*). Its dashes across the treeless sagebrush country of the West have been clocked at seventy miles an hour, and speeds of forty miles an hour for extended distances are not uncommon. But swiftness is not its only unique quality.

The pronghorn, a hoofed ruminant, is the world's only member of the *Antilocapridae* family. It has sometimes been called an antelope, but the Old World antelopes of the *Antilopinae* subfamily have solid, unforked horns that last a lifetime. It has been compared to a deer, but the *Cervidae* family have solid, branched antlers that are shed each year. The pronghorn has hollow horns set on bony cores, like the goat or sheep in the *Caprinae* subfamily, but is the only mammal in the world that sheds the outer covering of its horn each year. Further, it is the world's only animal with branching horns. Each black horn averages fifteen inches in length, with the longer prong pointing backward and the shorter pointing forward. Both sexes have horns.

A buck stands over 3 feet at the shoulder and weighs up to 140 pounds. A buff to reddish-brown coat of bristles covers his chunky body and slender legs. His white face is accented with a black nose, black sideburns, and protruding eyes. Most of his sides and underparts are white, and two dark bands emblazon his white throat. When trouble brews, long white hairs on his rump patch rise with his tail, thereby flashing a heliographic warning to compatriots as far as two miles away. The pronghorn's compulsive curiosity to investigate moving objects on the horizon sometimes leads him to the mercy of his enemies; extremely keen vision and swift legs cannot always make up for imprudent dallying.

Herds of seventy-five million pronghorns once grazed the open prairies of America, but by 1908 the number was reduced to twenty thousand. With careful management this graceful speedster was rescued from extinction and can now be hunted in some states during restricted seasons. The meat is held in high regard.

Dehydrated animal flesh has been important to many cultures. The Quechua Indians of South America called dried strips of meat *charqui,* from which comes our Yankee word *jerky.* The South African label is *biltong,* from the Dutch words *bil* (for buttock, the source of the meat) and *tong* (for tongue, the appearance of the meat). The Cree Indians of North America added melted fat and dried fruit to pulverized jerky and called it *pemmican.* Because pemmican provided a balanced ration, was easily stored and transported in hide pouches, kept almost indefinitely, and did not require cooking since in effect it had been cooked by sun, smoke,

Detail of Mimbres ceramic bowl with painting of a *pronghorn*.
From the Osborn ruin, New Mexico. About A.D. 1100. Diameter 10 inches.
Department of Anthropology, National Museum of Natural History,
Smithsonian Institution, Washington, #286,331.

and hot fat, it played a vital role in the early days of exploration and fur
trading in North America.

Jerky can be made from the flesh of bison, pronghorn, elk, deer, cow,
squirrel, rabbit, turkey, or salmon—to name but a few sources.

To make jerky, the Indians used to slice large pieces of meat into sheets
and hang them on willow frames to dry in the hot sun. An expert could cut
a whole hind quarter of buffalo into one massive sheet. Sometimes the
Indians also smoked the meat. The usual procedure today is to cut venison or
beef, with the grain, into strips about one-fourth inch thick, one inch wide,
and as long as practical. Only lean meat is used, because fat slows down
the drying. The strips can then be draped over a bush, laced onto sticks
over a slow-smouldering campfire (preferably aspen, hickory, or maple),
strung on twine in a shed, speared with kebob skewers across rafters in a
well-ventilated attic, or stretched across racks in a kitchen oven. When
necessary, nets are used to fend off flies or other insects. (It is said that
flies won't bother meat hung twenty feet or more above the ground.) Depending on the method and environ, the strips of meat glaze over, shrink,
and become brittle in two to four days. To hasten dehydration, the strips
can be sprinkled lightly with salt before hanging; or the strips can be
soaked for forty-eight hours in a brine made of one cup salt to eight cups
water (or dense enough to float an uncooked egg or potato) and blotted
dry before hanging. For flavor, strips can be soaked in Worcestershire
sauce, soy sauce, or liquid smoke.

Commercially-dehydrated meat contains no more than 10% fat. To speed drying, the meat is pre-cooked for thirty minutes at 165°F, which also kills pathogenic microorganisms and inactivates enzymes. It then is dried with forced air to a moisture content of less than 10%.

To make a shredded or powdered meat, the Indians used to spread the jerky on hides staked to the ground and then beat the strips with flails or ground them between flat stones. Nowadays a wide metal hammerhead and a strong wooden plank are likely home tools. Wild meat that is tough and strong-smelling can be tenderized and moderated in flavor by drying and pulverizing.

To make pemmican, the Indians mixed melted fat as well as rendered bone marrow with pulverized meat and then stirred in dried-and-pounded fruit such as wild grapes, cherries, berries, or rose hips. Sometimes herbs and maple sugar were also added. A favored proportion was five pounds of dried meat to four pounds of fat. In food value, a pound of pemmican equals from four to eight pounds of fresh meat, fish, or fowl. In 1840 the Hudson's Bay Company sold pemmican at two pence per pound.

To prepare jerky for eating, there are many choices. It can be sliced paper-thin before sautéing. It can be soaked in fresh water for a few hours, then wiped dry and cut into thin slices. It can be eaten uncooked.

To make a stew, melt 3 tablespoons butter. Add 1 bouillon cube and crush. Add 2 tablespoons flour plus 4 tablespoons dehydrated milk and mix well. Add sliced jerky and stir until the meat is well coated. Then slowly add 1 cup water, stirring all the while. Simmer until tender.

To make a soup on wilderness treks, powdered meat can be used to great advantage. If available, dehydrated tomatoes, carrots, potatoes, onions, and the like can be added. In their absence wild onion bulbs, fern fiddles, grape leaves, dandelion greens, or the bark from small pine trees can be substituted.

PRONGHORN JERKY CHILI

1 cup dried kidney beans

1 cup shredded jerky

¼ cup dehydrated onions

6 cups water

1 tablespoon chili powder

½ teaspoon salt

1 6-ounce can tomato paste or 2 ounces dehydrated tomato flakes

In large kettle combine beans, jerky, onions, water, chili powder, and salt. Bring to boil, cover, and simmer over low heat for 3 hours or until beans and meat are tender. Near end of cooking period, add tomato paste or dehydrated tomatoes. Add more water during cooking period if desired. Serves 3.

Brown-and-cream scroddled-ware creamer in the form of a *cow*.
From Bennington, Vermont, 1853–1858. Height 5 inches, length 6½ inches.
Wadsworth Atheneum, Hartford, #1918.1099.

COW

ARTISTS PAINTED BULLS on the slopes of the Lascaux caves in France and the Altamira caves in Spain over twenty-two thousand years ago, and about three thousand years ago sculptors carved the images of cattle on walls of Egyptian tombs so the animals' images would come alive in the hereafter to provide milk and meat for the kings buried within.

Our present-day Domestic Cow (*Bos taurus*) is descended from an ancient lineage that includes the extinct Aurochs (*B. primigenius*) and the Indian Zebu (*B. indicus*). There are 277 identifiable breeds raised for meat, dairy, and draft purposes today. A cow has hollow unbranched horns that are not shed, a four-sectioned stomach, cloven hoofs, a long tail, and in most cases short hair.

A *calf* is a young bovine, either male or female. A *bull* is an uncastrated mature male weighing 2,000 pounds or more; a *bullock* is a young bull. A *steer* is a castrated male. A steer two or three years old is an *ox*. A *heifer* is a young female that has not borne a calf. A *cow* is a mature female weighing from 1,000 to 1,700 pounds. Together they form a herd of *cattle*.

Beef cattle have heavy rectangular bodies with blocky necks and wide heads. Some outstanding meat breeds in the United States are the red-and-white Hereford, the black Aberdeen-Angus, the roan or red Shorthorn, and the gray, humped Brahman also called Zebu.

Dairy cattle have long heads and bodies that are lean except for their round stomachs encasing food that converts to milk. Common milk breeds in the United States are the black-and-white Holstein-Friesian and the brown Jersey.

Beef is meat derived from cattle nearly one year of age or older. *Veal* is meat derived from calves, generally up to fourteen weeks of age and more often from three to six weeks of age.

BEEF AND BULGUR IN VINE LEAVES

1 tablespoon butter	Melt butter in saucepan. Sauté wheat for ½ minute. Add liquid and salt. Cover pan, leaving lid slightly ajar for steam escapement. Simmer until liquid is absorbed by wheat—about 15 or 20 minutes.
½ cup cracked bulgur wheat	
1 cup consommé, or 1 cup water plus 1 bouillon cube	
½ teaspoon salt	
About 50 medium-sized fresh, young grape leaves	With sharp knife on cutting board or with scissors, snip away hub of tough fibers where each leaf joins stem. Place leaf in bottom of
Boiling water	

large bowl. Cover with boiling water. Add another leaf and a little more water. Repeat until half the leaves are immersed. Repeat process in another bowl with remaining ingredients. Drain and cool. (Leaves preserved in brine can be used by first freshening them in generous amount of water.)

1 pound lean ground beef, uncooked

1 large egg

1 clove garlic, crushed and minced

½ teaspoon dried rosemary, pulverized

½ teaspoon salt

¼ teaspoon ground black pepper

¼ cup dry white wine

Combine beef, egg, garlic, rosemary, salt, pepper, and cooked wheat. Spread leaf on countertop, shiny side down. In center of dull side of leaf, place spoonful of meat mixture shaped as long finger (larger and fatter if roll is to be served as entree, smaller and thinner if served as hors d'oeuvre). Fold double-rounded edge of leaf over meat and roll toward center; fold sides toward center; roll packet over remaining leaf-point to seal. Repeat until all meat is wrapped.

Butter a casserole and line with leaves, perhaps using tougher leaves or those that are torn. Place layer of rolls on bottom. Cover with a few leaves. Add more layers of rolls. Cover top layer with leaves and wine. Cover tightly. Bake in preheated 350°F oven for 45 minutes. Serve hot or cold, with preserved kumquats. Yield: about 36 rolls, each containing a level tablespoon of stuffing.

(Can be prepared in advance and reheated just before serving. Can also be frozen, either before or after initial baking.)

141

Porcelain dish decorated
with two *water buffaloes.*
From Ching-te-Chên, China,
eighteenth century.
Diameter 29 centimeters.
Collection Haags Gemeentemuseu
The Hague.

BISON

BUFFALO is the name commonly used in America for the mighty ox-like
Bison (*Bison bison*) that used to roam the prairies 60,000,000 strong from
the Appalachian Mountains to the Rockies. As many as 4,000,000 grazed in
one herd. This massive quadruped was a migrating "general store" that
provided all the merchandise a Plains Indian needed for a good life. Besides
yielding food and clothing, the animal's horns could be shaped into ladles,
the ribs made good sledrunners, the hoofs boiled down into glue, and the
hide converted to rope, blankets, trunks, shields, and tepees. With the west-
ward thrust of white settlers, an awesome slaughter of the animal gained
such force that by 1890 the stricken herds were reduced to less than 600
individuals. Only the most intensive conservation efforts rescued the vanish-
ing beast from extinction. Today over 10,000 plains bison live in the pro-

tection of government reservations and private ranches in the United States. Over 15,000 wood bison—the larger and darker Canadian subspecies—range in a national park south of Great Slave Lake.

The bison's shaggy head and high-humped shoulders taper into narrow hindquarters that are covered with short brown hair. Both bull and cow have coarse beards and unbranched crescent horns that are never shed. Their vicious tempers are easily aroused. A well-developed sense of smell and good hearing compensate for poor eyesight. A bull reaches full size in about 8 years, measures up to 12 feet in length and 6 feet in shoulder height, and weighs about a ton.

The larger European Bison (*B. bonasus*) is commonly called a Wisent. Few survive there today, although the herds are increasing under careful management.

The only true buffaloes of the world are native to Asia and Africa. The large-horned Water Buffalo (*Bubalus bubalis*) originated in India and is a common domesticated and sometimes-ill-tempered beast of burden in many warmer countries of Asia and the Mediterranean region. It stands 5 feet at the shoulders and weighs up to 1,700 pounds. Its rich milk is used for yoghurt and for cheeses such as mozzarella. The savage African Buffalo (*Syncerus caffer*) has never been tamed.

In 1935 charred bones of an extinct species of bison were uncovered at an ancient barbecue site in Colorado. They proved to be the remains of feasts held by Folsom men who hunted with stone-pointed javelins as the last glacial sheet receded.

To cook a stew, the American Indians sometimes hung a bison paunch on wooden stakes or pushed a fresh hide into a hole in the ground. Then they filled the hollow with water, meat, and hot stones. A hunting or war party on the march sometimes turned a freshly-slaughtered carcass on its back, filled the stomach cavity with water, meat, and hot stones, and thus used the unfortunate animal as a kettle in which to boil itself.

In *Butchering, Processing and Preservation of Meat*, Frank G. Ashbrook describes other cooking methods of the early days:

"The de'pouille, a fatty tissue lying along the backbone just under the hide and extending from shoulder blade to the last rib, was cut and pulled out all in one piece [by the Indians]. It was then dipped in hot fat for a short time and hung up inside the tepee. Here this choice morsel would dry and be smoked for a day or two. Cured in this manner, it kept indefinitely and was used principally as a substitute for bread.

"The flesh of the buffalo or bison, in good condition, is juicy and well flavored, and resembles that of beef. The tongue, in pioneer days, was deemed a delicacy, either roasted, boiled fresh, or cured and smoked. Smoked buffalo tongue was considered to surpass in flavor and texture that of the cow or steer. The hump of flesh covering the long spinal processes of the first dorsal vertebrae was also much esteemed. Fine-grained, mellow, and when partly salt-cured and sliced crosswise, it was considered as rich, tender, and luscious as tongue. Hump ribs and other choice cuts were roasted in the deep ashes of a fire, as were the marrow bones. These portions of the buffalo were most relished by the trappers, traders, pioneers, and travelers who came later." *

143

*©1955, reprinted by Van Nostrand Reinhold Company, New York

In the early 1870s when Dodge City, Kansas, was the buffalo capital of the world, a bison hide sold for $1.25, a three-pound tongue was worth 25¢, and hindquarters glutted the market at a penny a pound. By the time the buffalo nickel was minted in 1913, the flesh of the nearly-extinct animal was illegal to sell or buy. Today, however, regeneration of the species has been successful enough to enable government parks and private herdsmen to judiciously harvest two-year-olds and ship prime cuts to city markets.

BUFFALO TONGUE IN ASPIC

1 buffalo tongue (about 2 pounds)

2 carrots

2 stalks celery

2 small white onions

2 cloves garlic

1 bay leaf

15 whole peppercorns

1 tablespoon salt

Place tongue in large kettle. Add scraped carrots, broken celery stalks, peeled onions, peeled garlic, bay leaf, peppercorns, and salt. Cover with water. Bring to boil, then simmer for 3 hours or until tongue is tender. Remove tongue from broth. Strain broth; refrigerate until congealed fat can be removed. Reduce de-fatted stock to 3 cups by boiling. Trim bone and gristle from thick end of tongue; peel off skin. Dice lean meat into ¼-inch cubes, until 1½ cups are obtained; reserve.

¼ cup dry vermouth

2 tablespoons lemon juice

2 envelopes (2 tablespoons) unflavored gelatin powder

In pitcher or bowl, sprinkle gelatin powder over vermouth and lemon juice. Pour hot stock over gelatin mixture and stir until gelatin is thoroughly dissolved.

Pyrex mold, 4" x 8" x 3" (1½-quart capacity)

½ cup pitted green olives, sliced crosswise and blotted

½ cup coarsely-grated Swiss cheese

1 cup fresh watercress

Pour ½ cup stock into mold; chill until firm. Distribute olives on top of jelled layer; add ½ cup stock and chill until set. Distribute ¾ cup diced tongue over top; add ¾ cup stock and chill until set. Distribute cheese over top; add ½ cup stock and chill until set. Distribute ¾ cup diced tongue over top; add remaining stock. Chill several hours until aspic is thoroughly set. Arrange watercress on chilled serving platter. Unmold aspic onto bed of watercress. Serves 8.

Covered crystal bowl engraved with a *bison* leading a wild herd.
Glass design by Lloyd Atkins, engraving design by Bruce Moore, 1961.
Height 13 inches. Courtesy of Steuben Glass, New York.

Black-figured amphora depicting a *goat*.
From Attica, about 540 B.C.
Height 20 centimeters.
Courtesy of Museum of Fine Arts, Boston;
John Michael Rodocanachi Fund, #63.2664.

GOAT

"Poor man's cow!" Thus, since ancient times, is the reputation of the goat. And truly spoken, for the goat subsists on the coarsest of foods if necessary, resists disease, and relative to its size can give two or three times as much milk as a cow. Furthermore its sweet and highly-digestible milk makes very good cheeses and never harbors tubercular infection. This short-tailed ruminant with cloven hoofs and hollow horns is closely related to the sheep and thrives throughout most of the world. A male may be called a *buck, ram*, or *billy*; a female, a *doe* or *nanny*; and any goat under the age of one year, a *kid*. Both sexes have horns and are usually bearded. They live in small bands, although the males often prefer solitary trails.

The Domestic Goat (*Capra hircus*) is probably descended from the Persian wild goat with the same Latin name. Among the outstanding domestic breeds are the Swiss milk goat with pointed ears and the beardless Nubian milk goat with drooping ears.

The wild, beardless Alpine Ibex (*C. ibex*) living near perpetual snows of mountains of southern Europe is about 3 feet at the shoulder and weighs perhaps 240 pounds. Its coat is brown or gray, and its 30-inch horns are ridged on the front edges and arch backwards.

The shaggy white Rocky Mountain Goat (*Oreamnos americanus*) living on the treeless, wind-swept mountain peaks of northwestern North America is a goat-antelope. In regions of eternal ice it feeds on lichens, moss, flowers, and browse. A bearded male stands over 3 feet at its humped shoulder and weighs 300 pounds. Its black horns are slightly curved and may be a foot long. Black hoofs with spongy pads provide the suction-cup grip needed for perilous leaps up sheerest crags. The mountain goat's eyesight is keen

146

Gilded silver dish
showing King Peroz I (459–484)
hunting *ibexes* with bow and arrow.
From Persia, Sasanian period, fifth century.
Diameter 8⅜ inches.
The Metropolitan Museum of Art, New York;
Fletcher Fund, #34.33.

but does not always protect its life, for the animal erroneously believes that all trouble rises from below and fails to scout for hunters stalking from above. Avalanches of snow or rock, however, are its worst enemies. Though capable of climbing swiftly, the mountain goat normally moves slowly as befits a dignitary dwelling at the top of the world.

The beardless Chamois (*Rupicapra rupicapra*) of the loftiest mountains of Europe and Asia Minor is also a goat-antelope. The Pyrenees variety is called an izard; the Apennine variety, an abruzzi. A chamois' long brown coat changes to short gray as it shifts with the seasons from woodlands to snowfields. It stands 30 inches at the shoulder and weighs up to 90 pounds. Its 12-inch horns project straight upward to a tip that curves sharply backward.

Chamois and Rocky Mountain goat meats are valued for their mild, gamy character likened to venison. Most domestic goat meat is compared to mutton or lamb. Gourmet recipes concern themselves with kid, which up to the age of three or four months is tender and delicate.

147

GOAT KABOBS WITH GOOSEBERRY SAUCE

*Goat loin, about
3 pounds without bone*

1 tablespoon powdered ginger

2 teaspoons coriander

1 teaspoon salt

*1 teaspoon
powdered meat tenderizer*

*1 teaspoon
ground cumin seed*

½ teaspoon garlic salt

*½ teaspoon
finely-ground black pepper*

¼ teaspoon cayenne pepper

Remove and discard any sinew and fat. Cut meat into 1-inch cubes. Combine ginger, coriander, salt, tenderizer, cumin, garlic salt, black pepper, and cayenne pepper. Sprinkle spices over meat, then roll each piece in residue until all spices are absorbed. Place meat in glass, enameled, or stainless steel container.

1 cup distilled vinegar

2 tablespoons peanut oil

Pour vinegar and oil over meat. Compress meat so all pieces are submerged in liquid. Marinate for 2 hours.

1 tablespoon peanut oil

1 large yellow onion, diced

*1 large sweet
green pepper, diced*

Juice of 1 large lemon

2 tablespoons brown sugar

2 tablespoons peanut butter

¼ teaspoon salt

*1 can (15 ounces)
whole gooseberries
preserved in syrup*

Peanut oil for broiling

In thick-bottomed saucepan, over medium-low heat, sauté onions and green peppers in oil for about 5 minutes. Add lemon juice, brown sugar, peanut butter, and salt. Drain juice from can of gooseberries. Just before serving add gooseberries to saucepan, heating only until hot enough to serve; do not overcook causing fruit to become mushy.

After marination, drain meat and blot each piece with paper towel. Thread meat onto skewers. Brush with oil. Broil in oven or over charcoal broiler until browned as desired. Serve at once with hot gooseberry sauce and boiled lentils. Serves 6.

LEFT: *Mountain goat.* RIGHT: *Mountain sheep.* Painted on Mimbres pottery about A.D. 1100. Department of Anthropology, National Museum of Natural History, Smithsonian Institution *Miscellaneous Collections* 76:8, page 31 and 63:10, plate 2.

SHEEP

No ANIMAL LEAPS up and down rugged mountain slopes with as much speed and daring as the wild sheep. Not even the wild goat. The Bighorn Sheep (*Ovis canadensis*) lives in the most inaccessible western ranges of Canada, the United States, and northern Mexico. It is a stocky, beardless ruminant with hair like a deer rather than wool like a domestic sheep. The Rocky Mountain bighorn in the north has a brownish-gray coat with a white rump; the colors of the desert bighorn fade to paler tones in the south. The male, called a ram, stands over 3 feet at the shoulder and weighs as much as 300 pounds; the female, called a ewe, is considerably smaller. In bands as large as sixty they graze on grasses or browse on twigs, drinking frequently if water is available but surviving on moisture from cactus if necessary. A ram's massive, laterally-ribbed horns are never shed and must last the animal his entire lifetime. An elderly ram's horn can measure 40 inches along the outer curve and can spiral around more than 360 degrees; the tips may be deliberately broken off by the animal so his vision will not be blocked. His eyesight is impressively keen, in fact is said to be eight times better than a man's vision. The white Dall Sheep (*O. dalli*) is a smaller relative living in Alaska and northwestern Canada.

Man has been domesticating sheep for perhaps ten thousand years. Domestic Sheep (*O. aries*) are believed to be descended from the wild Mouflon (*O. musimon*) of Corsica and Sardinia. There are more than two hundred breeds today. One of the oldest and most widely distributed

Ceramic shaker in the form of a *sheep*.
From Asia Minor, seventh century B.C.
Soprintendenza alle Antichita, Florence, Italy, #4671.

throughout the world is the finely-fleeced Merino of Spanish origin. The medium-wool Hampshire is widespread in the United States where it is raised mainly for its superior meat.

The flesh of a sheep more than a year old is called *mutton*; it is dark pink with white fat. The flesh of a sheep less than a year old is called *lamb,* as is the animal itself; it is light pink with creamy-white or pinkish fat and is more tender and less strong in flavor than mutton. Most hunters consider the meat of wild mountain sheep far superior to that of domestic sheep, and they rate it the finest game meat in the world.

Haggis is a pudding made of the minced heart, liver, and lungs of a sheep, combined with onions, oatmeal, suet, and seasonings, and then boiled in the stomach of the animal. As national dish of Scotland, haggis is traditionally eaten on November 30, the feast day of St. Andrew who is patron saint of Scotland. It is typically served on a starched napkin with a side glass of whisky, accompanied by an escort of Scottish bagpipers. Today haggis can be bought in tins, or prepared according to simplified contemporary recipes, or made in the old-fashioned manner as follows:

SCOTTISH HAGGIS

(from Christian Isobel Johnstone's [Margaret Dods'] THE COOK AND HOUSEWIFE'S MANUAL. Edinburgh: Oliver and Boyd, 1828, third edition)

"Clean a sheep's pluck thoroughly. Make incisions in the heart and liver to allow the blood to flow out, and parboil the whole, letting the wind-pipe lie over the side of the pot to permit the phlegm and blood to disgorge from the lungs; the water may be changed after a few minutes' boiling for fresh water. A half-hour's boiling will be sufficient; but throw back the half of the liver to boil till it will grate easily; take the heart, the half of the liver, and part of the lights, trimming away all skins and black-looking parts, and mince them together. Mince also a pound of good beef-suet and four onions. Grate the other half of the liver. Have a dozen of small onions peeled and scalded in two waters to mix with this mince. Toast some oatmeal before the fire for hours, till it is of a light-brown colour and perfectly dry. Less than two tea-cupfuls of meal will do for this quantity of meat. Spread the mince on a board, and strew the meal lightly over it, with a high seasoning of pepper, salt, and a little cayenne, well mixed. Have a haggis-bag perfectly clean, and see that there be no thin part in it, else your whole labour will be lost by its bursting. Some cooks use two bags. Put in the meat with a half-pint of good beef-gravy, or as much strong broth, as will make it a thick stew. Be careful not to fill the bag too full, but allow the meat room to swell; and the juice of a lemon, or a little good vinegar; press out the air, and sew up the bag; prick it with a large needle when it first swells in the pot, to prevent bursting; let it boil slowly for three hours if large.

"This is a genuine Scotch haggis; the lemon and cayenne may be omitted, and instead of beef-gravy, a little of the broth in which the pluck was parboiled may be taken. A finer haggis may be made by parboiling and skinning sheep's tongues and kidneys, and substituting these minced for the most of the lights. There are, however, sundry modern refinements on the above receipt, such as eggs, milk, pounded biscuit, &c. &c.,—but these, by good judges, are not deemed improvements. Some cooks use the small fat tripes."

Wooden food bowl
in the form of a *pig*.
From the Admiralty Islands.
Trustees of the British Museum,
London, #7844.

BIBLIOGRAPHY

AARDVARK

ASHBROOK, FRANK G., *Butchering, Processing and Preservation of Meat*. New York: D. Van Nostrand Co., 1955, 318 pp.
  (information on sausagemaking)
  "Game or Hunters Sausage"

LAKE, ALEXANDER, *Hunter's Choice: True Stories of African Adventure*. Garden City, N. Y.: Doubleday & Co., 1954, 254 pp.
  "Aardvark Sausage"
  "Aardvark Curry"

ABALONE

GODDARD, WINIFRED M., *How to Cook Fish and Game*. Christchurch, N. Z.: Whitcombe & Tombs, 1966, 173 pp.
  "Creamed Paua, I and II"
  "Fried Paua"
  "Paua Soup, I and II"

MILLER, GLORIA BLEY, *The Thousand Recipes Chinese Cookbook*. New York: Atheneum, 1966, 927 pp.
  (information on soaking dried abalone and using canned abalone)
  "Abalone Soup"
  "Stir-Fried Abalone with Chicken and Asparagus"
  "Stir-Fried Abalone with Minced Pork"
  "Stir-Fried Abalone with Mixed Vegetables"
  "Stir-Fried Abalone with Mushrooms and Bamboo Shoots"
  "Stir-Fried Dried Abalone with Oyster Sauce"

SUNSET MAGAZINE, *Sunset Seafood Cook Book*. Menlo Park, Calif.: Lane Books, 1967, 96 pp.
  "Abalone Chowder"
  "Abalone Parmigiana"
  "Abalone Steaks with Egg Sauce"
  "Abalone Stew"

ALLIGATOR

BARR, BERYL, and BARBARA TURNER SACHS, *The Artists' & Writers' Cookbook*. Sausalito, Calif.: Angel Island Publications, 1961, 288 pp.
  "Coquille Crocodile—Frederick Franck"
  "Pâté Crocodile—Frederick Franck"

LAND, MARY, *Louisiana Cookery*. Baton Rouge: Louisiana State University Press, 1954, 376 pp.
  "Poached Alligator Tail"
  "Grilled 'Gator"

RAWLINGS, MARJORIE KINNAN, *Cross Creek Cookery*. New York: Charles Scribner's Sons, 1942, 230 pp.
  "Alligator-Tail Steak"

ARMADILLO

FEHRENBACH, LILLIAN, *The Pedernales Country Cookbook*. New York: The Macmillan Co.; London: Collier-Macmillan, 1968, 145 pp.
  "Fricassee of Armadillo"

LEAHY, CHARLES PARNELL [DON CARLOS], *Spanish-Mexican Cookbook*. Los Angeles: Charles Parnell Leahy, rev. 1951, 167 pp.
  "Armadillo in Red Chili Sauce"

MOREHEAD, JUDITH and RICHARD, *The Texas Wild Game Cookbook*. Austin, Tex.: The Encino Press, 1972, 81 pp.
  "Armadillo Barbecue Mop, Barbecue Sauce"
  "Armadillo Stuffed with Sweet Potato Compote"

BEAR

BATES, JOSEPH D., JR., *The Outdoor Cook's Bible*. Garden City, N. Y.: Doubleday & Co., 1963, 212 pp.
  "Bear Pot Roast"
  "Bear Steak"
  "Bear Steak Casserole"
  "Bear Stew"
  "Braised Bear"

DEGOUY, MASTER CHEF LOUIS P., *The Derrydale Game Cook Book*. New York: Greenberg, Publisher, 1937, 308 pp.
  "Bear au Grand Veneur"
  "Bear Fillet, Transylvanian Method"
  "Bear Steak Alexandre I, Russian Method"
  "Braised Bear Leg in Red Wine"
  "Braised Bear Liver, Russian Method"
  "Breast of Bear Sour Cream"
  "Fillet of Bear à la Zinoff"
  "Fillet of Bear Lumberjack, Canadian Recipe"
  "Fillet of Bear Piqué à la Broche"
  "Marinade for Bear—3"

BEAVER

ASHBROOK, FRANK G., and EDNA N. SATER, *Cooking Wild Game.* New York: Orange Judd Publishing Co., 1945.
　(directions for cleaning)
　"Barbecued Beaver"
　"Beaver Meat Loaf"
　"Beaver Meat Pie"
　"Beaver Pot Roast"
　"Beaver Stew"
　"Boiled Beaver Dinner, with Hot Horseradish Sauce"
　"Roast Beaver à la Michigan"
　. . . and other beaver recipes . . .

BOORMAN, SYLVIA, *Wild plums in brandy: A cookery book of wild foods in Canada.* Toronto: McGraw-Hill Co. of Canada, 1962, 176 pp.
　"Beaver Fricassee"

FLOOD, BARBARA, *Game in the Kitchen: Cookery for Nimrods, Anglers & Their Friends.* Barre, Mass.: Barre Publishers, 1968, 234 pp.
　"Roast Beaver"
　"Beaver Tail Soup"

BISON

ASHBROOK, FRANK G., *Butchering, Processing and Preservation of Meat.* New York: D. Van Nostrand Co., 1955, 318 pp.

Buffalo. San Jose, Calif.: Durham Meat Co., 12 pp.
　"Buffalo Stroganoff"
　"Cocktail Buffalo Meat Balls in Tomato-Wine Sauce"
　"Deviled Steak"
　"Epicurean Buffalo Roast"
　"Prime Ribs Barbecued in Salt Jacket"
　. . . and other buffalo recipes; cooking tips . . .

Gourmet Cookbook, The. New York: Gourmet Distributing Corp., Volume I, 1950, 781 pp.
　"Bison or Buffalo Pies (Pâtés de Bison Bourgeoise)"
　"Fillet of Bison Gamekeeper Manner"
　Volume II, 1957, 753 pp.
　"Braised Buffalo Hump with Sour Cream"
　"Broiled Buffalo Steaks"
　"Potted Bison (Terrine de Bison Américain)"

BLACKBIRD

BANDERA LIBRARY ASSOCIATION, *Cooking Recipes of the Pioneers.* Bandera, Tex.: Frontier Times, 1936, 30 pp.
　"Blackbird Pie"

HOWE, ROBIN, and PAULINE ESPIR, *Sultan's Pleasure: and Other Turkish Recipes.* New York: A. A. Wyn, 1953, 152 pp.
　"Blackbird Stew (Karataruk Yahnisi)"

McGRAIL, JOIE and BILL, *The Catch And The Feast.* New York: Weybright and Talley, 1969, 196 pp.
　"Uccelletti with Black Olives"

CAMEL

MONTAGNÉ, PROSPER, *Larousse Gastronomique: The Encyclopedia of Food, Wine & Cookery.* Paris: Augé, Gillon, Hollier-Larousse, Moreau et Cie (Librairie Larousse), 1938. New York: Crown Publishers, 1961, 1101 pp.
　"Camel Couscous (Arab cooking)"
　"Camel Escalopes with Pimentos and Aubergines"
　"Camel's Feet à la Vinaigrette"
　"Roast Camel's Fillet"
　"Roast Camel's Hump"
　"Camel's Paunch à la Marocaine"
　"Camel Pilaf"
　"Ragout of Camel with Tomato Sauce"
　"Camel Ribs with Rice"

SHORT, DOROTHY, *Camel Land Cookery* [Afghanistan]. Beirut?: © Dorothy Short, 1964, unpaged.
　"Camel's Leg Roast"
　"Camel Steak"

CHICKEN

ARESTY, ESTHER B., *The Delectable Past.* New York: Simon & Schuster, 1964, 255 pp.
　"Apician Dilled Chicken (In Pullo Elixo Ius Crudum)" (1st century)
　"Capon with Lemon Sauce" (1597)
　"Will Rabisha's Green Chicken" (1661)
　. . . and other chicken recipes . . .

DAVIS, LUCILLE (Su Chung), *Court Dishes of China: The Cuisine of the Ch'ing Dynasty.* Rutland, Vt. and Tokyo: Charles E. Tuttle Co., 1965, 243 pp.
　"Beggar's Chicken (baked in clay)"
　"Brocade-Like Array of Chicken, Pork, Prawns, and Vegetables"
　"Chicken and Bean Curd Skin"
　"Chicken and Cucumber with Sauce"
　"Chicken and Mushroom Filling for Miniature Dumplings"
　"Chicken, Bamboo, and Mushroom Soup"
　"Clear Chicken Soup with Jasmine Petals"
　"Fried Chicken Gizzard with Walnuts"
　"Julienned Chicken Simmered with Chrysanthemum Petals"
　"Smoked Chicken with Chinese Cabbage"
　. . . and other chicken recipes . . .

WILSON, CHRISTINE, *Secrets of Eastern Cooking.* New York: Hastings House, 1966, 233 pp.
　"Chicken Curry: Burmese, Celanese, Indian, Malayan, Rangoon"
　"Chicken Liver Sambal"
　"Chicken Parsi Style"
　"Chicken Sukiyaki"
　"Chicken Tundoori"
　"Circassian Chicken"
　. . . and other chicken recipes . . .

CLAM

DAY, BUNNY, *Catch 'em and Cook 'em.* Garden City, N.Y.: Doubleday & Co., 1961, 114 pp.
　(information on digging and cleaning)
　"Ben's Clam Appetizers"
　"Mama Georgie's Clam Fritters"
　"Peconic Stuffed Clams"
　"Steamer Chowder"
　. . . and other clam recipes . . .

FISH AND WILDLIFE SERVICE, *How to Cook Clams,* test kitchen series no. 8. Washington, D.C.: U.S. Dept. of the Interior, 1954, 13 pp.
　(directions for shucking)
　"Manhattan Clam Chowder"
　"Sour Cream Clam Pie"
　. . . and other clam recipes . . .

McCLANE, A. J., ed., *McClane's Standard Fishing Encyclopedia.* New York: Holt, Rinehart and Winston, 1965, 1057 pp.
　(information on quahaugs, sea clams, butter clams, razor clams, steamer clams, geoducks, and others)
　"Clam Hash"
　"Deviled Clams"
　"New England Clam Chowder"
　. . . and other clam recipes . . .

CONCH

BAKER, CHARLES H., JR., *The Gentleman's Companion: Volume I, Being An Exotic Cookery Book, or, Around the World with Knife, Fork and Spoon.* New York: The Derrydale Press, 1939, 220 pp.
　"A Nassau Curry of Conchs"
　"Bahama, & Florida Keys, Raw Conch Salad—sometimes called Conch Souse"
　"Bahama Conch Chowder"
　"Smothered Conch, Ernest Hemingway"

154

DAVIS, NORMA A., *Trade Winds Cookery: Tropical Recipes for All America*. Richmond, Va.: The Dietz Press, 1956, 215 pp.
"Conch Crisp (Key West)"
"Conch Fritters"
"Conch Salad"
"Conch Soup"
"Conch Souse (British West Indies)"
"Fried Conchs"
"Key West Conch Chowder"

COW

BECK, SIMONE; LOUISETTE BERTHOLLE; and JULIA CHILD, *Mastering the Art of French Cooking*. New York: Alfred A. Knopf, 1961, 684 pp.
"Beef and Onions Braised in Beer (Carbonnades à la Flamande)"
"Boiled Beef with Pork, Chicken, Sausage, and Vegetables (Potée Normande, Pot-au-Feu)"
"Braised Sweetbreads with Brown Mushroom Sauce (Ris de Veau Braisés à l'Italienne)"
"Filet Steaks with Artichoke Hearts, Foie Gras, Truffles, and Madeira Sauce (Tournedos Rossini)"
"Pan-broiled Steak, with Shallot and White Wine Sauce (Bifteck Sauté Bercy)"
"Sautéed Veal Scallops with Brown Tarragon Sauce (Escalopes de Veau à l'Estragon)"
"Veal Chops Braised with Herbs (Côtes de Veau aux Herbes)"
"Veal Gratinéed with Onions and Mushrooms (Veau Prince Orloff)"
"Veal Kidneys in Red Wine Sauce with Marrow (Rognons de Veau à la Bordelaise)"
. . . and other beef and veal recipes . . .

CLAIBORNE, CRAIG, *The New York Times Cook Book*. New York: Harper & Row, Publishers, 1961, 717 pp.
"Beef Roast: high- and low-temperature methods"
"Boeuf Bourguignon I, II"
"Budapest Beef Goulash I, II"
"Osso Buco"
"Veal Birds: with Chicken Livers; Italian"
"Veal Schnitzel with Kidneys"
. . . and other beef and veal recipes . . .

FRANK, JEANNETTE, *The Modern Meat Cookbook*. New York: The Bobbs-Merrill Co., 1958, 1969, 452 pp.
(discussion of meat grading, nutrition, freezing, basic cooking methods, standard cuts and their characteristics, tenderizers, etc.)
"Carpetbag Steak with Oyster Stuffing"
"Rolled Flank Steak Polenta"
. . . and other beef and veal recipes . . .

CRAB

FISH AND WILDLIFE SERVICE, *How to Cook Crabs*, test kitchen series no. 10. Washington, D.C.: U.S. Dept. of the Interior, 1956, 14 pp.
(directions for cleaning)
"Chesapeake Bay Crab Cakes"
"Crab Jambalaya"
"Crab Louis"
"Crab Salad in Aspic Rings"
. . . and other crab recipes . . .

GIBBONS, EUELL, *Stalking the Blue-Eyed Scallop*. New York: David McKay Co., 1964, 332 pp.
(information on catching blue crab, rock crab, jonah crab, southern stone crab, lady or sand crab, green crab, dungeness crab, red or sea crab, and others.)
"Soft-Shelled Crabs—how to clean, fry, broil, or sauté"
"Southern Crab Gumbo"
. . . and other crab recipes . . .

SARVIS, SHIRLEY, *Crab & Abalone*. New York: The Bobbs-Merrill Co., 1968, 160 pp.
"Avocado Crab Crêpes, Imperial Dynasty"
"Cantonese Ginger Crab with Green Vegetables"
"Coconut Crab Soup"
"Crab and Eggplant Chablis"
"Crab and Macadamia Tropical Platter"
"Crab *Chawan Mushi*"
"Hogan's All-Crab Cioppino"
"Sherry Crab in Cream—Parmesan Popovers"
. . . and other crab recipes . . .

CRANE

AUSTIN, THOMAS, *Two Fifteenth Century Cookery Books*. London: Early English Text Society, 1888, unpaged.
"Display That Crane"
"Dysmembre That Heron"

FITZGIBBON, THEODORA, *Game Cooking: A Collection of Recipes with a Dictionary of Rare Game*. London: Andre Deutsch, 1963, 254 pp.
"Heron Pie or Pudding"
"Roast Cormorant"

DEER

BARDWELL, FLORA; J. B. LOW; and ETHELWYN B. WILCOX, *Venison: Field Care and Cooking*. Salt Lake City: Utah State Division of Fish and Game, 1968, 32 pp.
"Kennicott Venison Stew"
"Roast Venison with Marinade"
"Venison Mincemeat"
"Venison Oriental Steak"
"Venison Swiss Steak Variations"
. . . and other venison recipes . . .

GORTON, AUDREY ALLEY, *The Venison Book: How to Dress, Cut Up and Cook Your Deer*. Brattleboro, Vt.: The Stephen Greene Press, 1957, 78 pp.
"Cornish Pasties"
"Marinades—5"
"Stuffed Venison Heart"
"Venison Stroganoff"
. . . and other venison recipes . . .

DOVE

LEVI, WENDELL MITCHELL, *The Pigeon*. Sumter, S.C.: Levi Publishing Co., 1941, 667 pp.
"Pigeon Salad"
"Roasted Old Pigeon"
"Roasted Stuffed Squabs"
"Smothered Squab Southern Style"
. . . and other squab and pigeon recipes . . .

POLLARD, MAJOR HUGH B. C., *The Sportsman's Cookery Book*. London: Country Life, 1926, 156 pp.
"American Pigeon"
"Fried Pigeon"
"Pigeon and Asparagus"
"Pigeon Pie"
"Pigeon Pudding"
"Squabs (Nestling Pigeons)"
. . . and other pigeon recipes . . .

STEINDLER, GERALDINE, *Shooter's Bible Game Cookbook*. S. Hackensack, N.J.: Shooter's Bible; Toronto, Ont.: Ryerson Press, 1965, 208 pp.
"Braised Pigeons in Italian Sauce"
"Breast of Pigeon with Wine Sauce"
"Doves en Casserole"
"Roast Squab"

WAYLAND, VIRGINIA and HAROLD, *Of Carving, Cards and Cookery*. Arcadia, Calif.: Raccoon Press, 1962, unpaged.
"To Boil Pigeons in the French Fashion"

DUCK

BARNETT, HARRIET and JAMES, *Game and Fish Cookbook: Including Recipes from* Game Cookery *by Raymond Camp.* New York: Grossman Publishers, 1968, 162 pp.
  "Bahamas Duck"
  "Barbecued Duck"
  "Broiled Duck, Ray Camp"
  "Cacciatore Garigliano"
  "Currituck Duck"
  "Duck Soup"
  "Mallard Waidmanns (Hunter Style)"
  "Marinated Duck, Italian Style"
  "Pressed Duck"
  "Roasted Duck Italian"
  "Spitted Duck"
  "Wild Duck on Top of the Stove"

CHU, GRACE ZIA, *The Pleasures of Chinese Cooking.* New York: Simon and Schuster, 1962, 240 pp.
  "Canton Roast Duck"
  "Nanking Spiced Duck"
  "Peking Duck"
  "Szechuen Duck"

EEL

FREUCHEN, DAGMAR, with WILLIAM CLIFFORD, *Cookbook of the Seven Seas.* New York: M. Evans and Co., 1968, 256 pp.
  "Broiled Eels"
  "Eels in Red Wine (Lamproie Bordelaise)"
  "Fried Eels"

MARKEVITCH, MARIE ALEXANDRE, *The Epicure in Imperial Russia.* San Francisco: The Colt Press, 1941, 102 pp.
  "Stuffed Eel"

MAY, ROBERT, *The Accomplisht Cook, or the Art & Mystery of Cookery: Wherein the whole* ART *is revealed in a more easie and perfect Method, than hath been publisht in any language. Expert and ready Ways for the Dressing of all Sorts of* FLESH, FOWL, *and* FISH, *with variety of* SAUCES *proper for each of them; and how to raise all manner of Pastes; the best Directions for all sorts of Kickshaws, also the Terms of* CARVING *and* SEWING. *An exact account of all Dishes for all Seasons of the Year, with other A-la-mode Curiosities. Approved by the fifty five years Experience and Industry of* ROBERT MAY, *in his Attendance on several Persons of Great Honour.* London, Eng.: Printed for Obadiah Blagrave at the Bear and Star in St. Pauls Church-Yard, 1685, 461 pp.
  "To boil Eels to be eaten hot"
  . . . and 34 other eel recipes . . .

ELEPHANT

BAKER, SIR SAMUEL W., *The Nile Tributaries of Abyssinia.* London: Macmillan and Co., 1867, 596 pp.

CLOS-JOUVE, HENRY, *La Cuisine de Bacchus.* Paris: Solar, 1974. "Pieds d' Éléphant"

GILLHAM, C. E., "Mastodon and Other Rare Meats." *Field and Stream,* October 1968, p. 68.

ELK

BROWN, HELEN EVANS, and PHILIP S. BROWN, *The Cookout Book: Selected recipes from America's Cookout Championships . . . held in Hawaii, with an introduction to the techniques of barbecue cooking and entertaining by the Browns.* Los Angeles: The Ward Ritchie Press, 1961, 144 pp.
  "Colorado Hunting Camp Elk Steak"

MACILQUHAM, FRANCES, *Canadian Game Cookery.* Toronto: McClelland and Stewart, 1966, 214 pp.
  (field care of big game; home care, cutting and freezing)
  "Collared Flank of Corned Elk"
  "Elk Collops"
  "Filet Mignon of Elk with Butterballs"
  . . . and other elk recipes . . .

FROG

KIMBALL, YEFFE, and JEAN ANDERSON, *The Art of American Indian Cooking.* Garden City, N.Y.: Doubleday & Co., 1965, 215 pp.
  "Batter-Fried Frogs Legs"

ROMBAUER, IRMA S., and MARION ROMBAUER BECKER, *Joy of Cooking.* Indianapolis, Ind.: The Bobbs-Merrill Co., 1962, 849 pp.
  "Braised Frog Legs"
  "Deep-Fat Fried Frog Legs"
  "Frog Legs Forestière"
  "Frog Legs in Mushroom Sauce"

GOAT

CLEVELAND, BESS A., *Alaskan Cookbook.* Berkeley, Calif.: Howell-North, 1960, 164 pp.
  "Mountain Goat Stew with Dumplings"
  "Roast Loin of Mountain Goat"
  "Talkeetna Mountain Goat Roast"

KHAYAT, MARIE KARAM, and MARGARET CLARK KEATINGE, *Food from the Arab World.* Beirut, Lebanon: Khayat's 1959, 163 pp.
  "Roast Stuffed Kid (Saudi Arabia)"

LO PINTO, MARIA, *The Art of Regional Italian Cooking.* Garden City, N.Y.: Doubleday & Co., 1963, 350 pp.
  "Kid or Lamb Lucania Style (Capretto alla Lucania)"
  "Mountain Antelope Piedmontese Style (Chamois alla Piedmontese)"
  with "Piquant Sauce Tiberius"

STOKER, CATHARINE ULMER, *Concha's Mexican Kitchen Cook Book.* San Antonio, Tex.: The Naylor Co., 1946, 244 pp.
  "Roasted Goat with Sauce (Cabrito Asado Con Salsa)"
  "Stewed Goat with Gravy (Cabrito Con Salsa)"

GOOSE

BEARD, JAMES, *Fowl and Game Cookery.* New York: M. Barrows & Co., 1944, 196 pp.
  "Blanquette of Goose"
  "Golden State Goose"
  "New Year's Eve Goose"
  "Roasting a Goose"
  . . . and other goose recipes . . .

LAUGHTON, CATHRINE C., *Mary Cullen's Northwest Cook Book.* Portland, Oreg.: Binfords & Mort, Publishers, 1946, 340 pp.
  "Roast Domestic Goose"
  "Stuffings: Bread, Giblets, Cornbread, Apple, Oyster"
  "Roast Wild Goose"

MACILQUHAM, FRANCES, *Canadian Game Cookery.* Toronto: McClelland and Stewart, 1966, 214 pp.
  (discussion of care and dressing of gamebirds)
  "Roast Canadian Goose, White Front"
  . . . goose marinated, pickled, smoked, planked, stuffed, casseroled, loafed . . . and other goose recipes . . .

GRASSHOPPER

BODENHEIMER, F. S., *Insects as Human Food.* The Hague: Dr. W. Junk, Publisher, 1951, 352 pp.

CLAUSEN, LUCY W., *Insect Fact and Folklore.* New York: The Macmillan Co., 1954, 194 pp.

GERARD, W. R., "Entomophagy," *Poughkeepsie Society of Natural History* 1 (1875): 17–31.

JOHN, FOURTH MARQUIS OF BUTE, K.T., *Moorish Recipes.* Edinburgh, London: Oliver and Boyd, 1954, 80 pp.
  "Locust Bread (Khubz el Jarade)"

TORRE-BUENO, J. R. DE LA, "Why Not Eat Insects?" *Bulletin of the Brooklyn Entomological Society* 39 (1944):122–131.

GUINEA FOWL

FitzGibbon, Theodora, *Game Cooking: A Collection of Recipes with a Dictionary of Rare Game*. London: Andre Deutsch, 1963, 254 pp.
    "Guinea Fowl Chasseur"
    "Guinea Fowl Contadini"
    "Guinea Fowl with Red Wine and Garlic Sauce"
    "Sweet and Sour Guinea Fowl"
    "Turkish Guinea Fowl"

Gourmet Cookbook, The. New York: Gourmet Distributing Corp., Vol. I, 1950, 781 pp.
    "Breast of Guinea Hen en Casserole Connaisseur"
    "Breast of Guinea Hen Vendangeurs"
    "Roast Stuffed Guinea Hen Bourgeoise"
    Vol. II, 1957, 753 pp.
    "Baby Guinea Hens with Cherries (Pintadeaux aux Cerises)"
    "Breast of Guinea Hen Perigourdine (Suprêmes de Pintade Périgourdine)"
    "Breast of Guinea Hen Smitane"
    "Casserole of Guinea Hens (Pintades en Cocotte)"
    "Guinea Hen Chimay, Noodle Stuffing"

HALIBUT

Mellinkoff, Ruth, *The Uncommon Cook Book*. Los Angeles: The Ward Ritchie Press, 1968, 277 pp.
    "A Rococo Coral and White Paté of the Sea"
    "Halibut Mousse"
    "Sherried Halibut for Harried Housewives"
    "Triton's Trick, an Easy but Splendid Way with Halibut"

Morris, Dan, and Matilda Moore, *The Savor of the Sea: A Complete Seafood Cookbook*. New York: The Macmillan Co., 1966, 341 pp.
    "Halibut and Shrimp Salad"
    "Halibut Loaf"
    . . . and other halibut recipes . . .

HOG

DeGouy, Master Chef Louis P., *The Derrydale Game Cook Book*. New York: Greenberg, Publisher, 1937, 308 pp.
    "Braised Fillet of Wild Boar in Cider"
    "Braised Haunch of Wild Boar, Prince de Chimay"
    "Braised Hind Leg of Wild Boar, German Method"
    "Braised Shoulder of Wild Boar, Russian Style"
    "Breast of Wild Boar"
    "Grilled Fillet of Wild Boar, Moscovite"
    "Jugged Shoulder of Wild Boar in Red Wine"
    "Roast Chestnut-Stuffed Baby Wild Boar"
    "Wild Boar Cutlet à la Moldave"
    "Wild Boar Cutlet Flemish Method"
    "Wild Boar Cutlet Saint Marc"
    "Wild Boar Head in Loaf (Hure de Sanglier)"
    "Wild Boar Leg Agra Dolce, Italian Recipe"
    . . . and other boar recipes . . .

Grigson, Jane, *The Art of Charcuterie: Or—how to cook all parts of the pig in the grand manner of the French charcuteries*. New York: Alfred A. Knopf, 1968, 349 pp.

Harwood, Jim, and Ed Callahan, *Soul Food Cook Book*. Concord, Calif.: Nitty Gritty Productions, 1969, 210 pp.
    "Chitt'lins"
    "Hogmaw"
    "Hogshead Cheese"
    "Pig's Feet"
    "Snout"
    "South Carolina Scrapple"
    . . . and other pork recipes . . .

Miller, Jill Nhu Huong, *Vietnamese Cookery*. Rutland, Vt. and Tokyo: Charles E. Tuttle Co., 1968, 118 pp.
    "Carmelized Pork"
    "Noodle Salad-Soup (Mi Quang)"
    "Pork and Coconut Water Stew"
    "Pork, Shrimp and Vegetable Pancake-Omelet (Banh Xeo)"

    "Saffron Eggplant with Pork"
    "Stuffed Cucumber Slices"
    "Trotting Bamboo Stew"
    . . . and other pork recipes . . .

Wall, Roy, *Fish and Game Cookery*. New York: M. S. Mill Co., 1945, 218 pp.
    "Broiled Chops of Peccary, Wild Pig, Musk Hog or Javelina"
    "Roasted Ham of Peccary"

IGUANA

Graham, Gladys R., *Tropical Cooking: A Handbook of Tropical Foods and How to Use Them*. Panama, Repub. Pan.: The Panama American Press, 1947, 130 pp.
    "Iguana à la King"
    "Iguana Pie"
    "Smothered Iguana"

Harney, William Edward, with Patricia Thompson, *Bill Harney's Cook Book*. Melbourne, Austral.: Lansdowne Press, 1960, 89 pp.
    (directions for cleaning)
    "Baked Goanna"

Morphy, Countess, *Recipes of All Nations*. New York: William H. Wise & Co., 1935, 821 pp.
    "Fricasée of Iguana (from Guinea, Africa)"

Trader Vic's Kitchen Kibitzer. Garden City, N.Y.: Doubleday & Co., 1952: 223 pp.
    "Braised Iguana with Vegetables"

KANGAROO

Alexandre Dumas' Dictionary of Cuisine, edited, abridged and translated by Louis Colman from *Le Grand Dictionnaire de Cuisine* (Paris, 1873). New York: Simon and Schuster, 1958, 282 pp.
    "Sautéed Kangaroo Fillet"

Mason, Anne, *A Treasury of Australian Cooking*. London: Andre Deutsch, 1962, 255 pp.
    "Kangaroo Tail Soup—I and II"

LOBSTER

Beard, James, *Fish Cookery*. Boston: Little, Brown and Co., 1954, 460 pp.
    "Lobster Archduke"
    "Lobster Bisque"
    "Lobster Fra Diavolo"
    "Lobster North African"
    "Lobster Soufflé, Plaza Athenée"
    . . . and other lobster recipes . . .

Dueland, Joy V., *The Book of the Lobster*. New York: Charles Scribner's, 1974
    . . . 43 lobster recipes . . .

Montagné, Prosper, *Larousse Gastronomique: The Encyclopedia of Food, Wine & Cookery*. Paris: Augé, Gillon, Hollier-Larousse, Moreau et Cie (Librairie Larousse), 1938. New York: Crown Publishers, 1961, 1101 pp.
    "Crayfish Flan with Cheese"
    "Crayfish Mousse à l'Ancienne
    "Crayfish Tail Gratin à la Facon de Maître La Planche"
    "Lobster à la Franco-Américaine"
    "Lobster à la Parisienne"
    "Lobster Brillat-Savarin"
    "Lobster Newburg"
    . . . and other crayfish and lobster recipes . . .

MOOSE

Ellis, Eleanor A., ed., *Northern Cookbook*. Ottawa, Ont.: Queen's Printer, 1967, 358 pp.
    "Jellied Moose Nose"
    "Moose Head Cheese"
    "Moose Mincemeat"
    "Stuffed Moose Heart"
    . . . and other moose recipes . . .

UNIVERSITY OF ALASKA COOPERATIVE EXTENSION SERVICE, *The Hunter Returns After the Kill.* College, Alaska: University of Alaska and U.S. Dept. of Agriculture, 1963, 19 pp.
    "Corned Moose"
    "Pressed Corned Moose"
    "Cold Brined Jerky"
    "Hot Brined Jerky"
    . . . and other moose recipes . . .

MOUNTAIN LION

ANGIER, BRADFORD, *Wilderness Cookery.* Harrisburg, Pa.: The Stackpole Co., 1961, 256 pp.
    "Lynx Fricassee"

CARHART, ARTHUR H., *The Outdoorsman's Cookbook.* New York: The Macmillan Co., 1944, 1955, 211 pp.
    (suggestions for cleaning and cooking puma)

GRAHAM, GLADYS R., *Tropical Cooking: A Handbook of Tropical Foods and How to Use Them.* Panama, Repub. of Pan.: The Panama American Press, 1947, 130 pp.
    "Jaguar, Leopard, Ocelot, Panther, Puma—fricassee"

LAKE, ALEXANDER, *Hunter's Choice: True Stories of African Adventure.* Garden City, N.Y.: Doubleday & Co., 1954, 254 pp.
    "Jugged Lion, Omohundro"

MUSSEL

BROWN, HELEN EVANS, *Shrimp and Other Shellfish Recipes,* Los Angeles: The Ward Ritchie Press, 1966, 152 pp.
    "Curried Mussels"
    "Mussels Poulette"
    "Mussels Vinaigrette"
    "Piquant Baked Mussels"
    "Steamed Mussels"

GIBBONS, EUELL, *Stalking the Blue-Eyed Scallop.* New York: David McKay Co., 1964, 332 pp.
    (information on gathering and cleaning)
    "French Mussels"
    "Fried Mussels"
    "Mussels with Scrambled Eggs"
    . . . and other mussel recipes . . .

HALE, WILLIAM HARLAN, *The Horizon Cookbook: an Illustrated History of Eating and Drinking through the Ages.* New York: American Heritage Publishing Co., 1968, 768 pp.
    "Mussels with Sweet Herbs (after *moules marinières* in Robert Day's *The Accomplisht Cook,* London, 1660)"
    "Stuffed Mussels (Midye Dolmasi)"

NORMAN, BARBARA, *The Spanish Cookbook.* New York: Atheneum, 1966, 245 pp.
    (information on cleaning)
    "Cold Mussels with Almond Sauce"
    "Cold Mussels with Lemon Dressing"
    "Mussels in Tomato Sauce"

OCTOPUS

CLAIBORNE, CRAIG, *The New York Times Menu Cook Book.* New York: Harper & Row, Publishers, 1966, 727 pp.
    "Italian-Style Squid with Tomatoes"
    "Squid Stir-Fried Chinese Style"
    "Stuffed Squid"

DAVID, ELIZABETH, *Mediterranean Food.* Harmondsworth, Eng. and Baltimore, Md.: Penguin Books, 1955, 1965, 203 pp.
    (directions for cleaning)
    "Civet of Inkfish"
    "Grilled Calamari (cuttlefish, inkfish, squid)"
    . . . and other cephalopod recipes . . .

KERR, GRAHAM, *The Graham Kerr Cookbook,* by the Galloping Gourmet. Garden City, N.Y.: Doubleday & Co., 1969, 284 pp.
    (directions for cleaning)
    "Lyall Bay Casserole"
    "Strip Dip"

LANE, FRANK W., *Kingdom of the Octopus: The Life History of the Cephalopoda.* New York: Sheridan House, 1960, 300 pp.
    "Octopus Hors d'oeuvre"
    . . . and other cephalopod recipes . . .

OPOSSUM

HARTMAN, CARL G., *Possums.* Austin, Tex.: University of Texas Press, 1952, 174 pp.
    "Possum and Taters, Mississippi Hillbilly Style (Mrs. F.V.B.D.)"
    "Possum Stuffed with Chinquapins, Civil War Recipe (Mrs. F.V.B.D.)"
    "Roast Possum with Sassafras (Mrs. F.V.B.D.)"
    "Alma's Recipe for Possum (Mrs. S. R. Dull, *Southern Cooking*)"
    . . . and other opossum recipes . . .

KEEFE, JAMES F., *The World of the Opossum.* Philadelphia: J. B. Lippincott Co., 1967, 144 pp.
    "Opossum and Sweet Potatoes (Mrs. A. A. Heinze)"
    "Possum and Sweet Taters (Art Pugh)"
    "Roast Opossum Supreme (Judge Thomas V. Proctor)"

OSTRICH

DEVILLIERS, S. J. A., *Cook and Enjoy It: South African Cookery Manual.* Johannesburg, U.S.A.: Central News Agency, 1961, 531 pp.
    "Creamed Ostrich Egg"
    "Scrambled Ostrich Egg"

FLOWER, BARBARA, and ELISABETH ROSENBAUM, *The Roman Cookery Book: a critical translation of The Art of Cooking, by Apicius,* Rome, first century. London: G. G. Harrap, 1958, 240 pp.
    "Sauces for Boiled Ostrich"

OYSTER

BOLITHO, HECTOR, ed., *The Glorious Oyster: Its history, in Rome and Britain; what various writers and poets have said in its praise; together with chapters by Maurice Burton, D.Sc., on the 'Reproduction and Growth' of oysters, 'Their Enemies', their 'Anatomy and Physiology', and their 'Culture'; and a chapter on 'Oysters, Raw and Cooked' by W. A. Bentley.* New York: Horizon Press, 1961, 174 pp.
    . . . 39 oyster recipes . . .

CANNON, POPPY, and PATRICIA BROOKS, *The Presidents' Cookbook: Practical Recipes from George Washington to the Present.* New York: Funk & Wagnalls, 1968, 545 pp.
    "Brown Oyster Stew"
    "Fried Oysters Without Oysters"
    "Opelousas Oyster Gumbo"
    "Pickled Oysters"
    . . . and other oyster recipes . . .

STANFORTH, DEIRDRE, *The New Orleans Restaurant Cookbook.* Garden City, N.Y.: Doubleday & Co., 1967, 240 pp.
    "Oyster and Artichoke Casserole (Pontchartrain)"
    "Oysters Beach House (Masson's)"
    "Oysters Brochette (Antoine's)"
    "Oysters Carnaval (Dunbar's)"
    "Oysters Rockefeller (Commander's)"
    "Oysters Roffignac (Brennan's)"
    . . . and other oyster recipes . . .

PEACOCK

AUSTIN, THOMAS, *Two Fifteenth-Century Cookery-Books.* London: Early English Text Society, 1888.
    "Pecok rosted"

SMITH, HENRY, *The Master Book of Poultry and Game.* London: Practical Press, 1949, 320 pp.
    "To Truss a Peahen"
    "Peahen Roasted"

SOYER, ALEXIS, *The Pantropheon: or, History of Food, and Its Preparation, from the Earliest Ages of the World.* Boston: Ticknor, Reed, & Fields, 1853, 472 pp.
    "Peacock of Samos"

PHEASANT

Botsford, Harry, *Fish and Game Cook Book*. New York: Cornell Maritime Press, 1947, 290 pp.
  "Mexican Pheasant"
  "Pheasantburgers"
  "Pheasant Cacciatore"
  "Pheasant Pie"
  "Pheasant Potatoes"
  "Pheasant-Rice Casserole"
  "Pheasant—South Dakota Style"
  "Pheasant Tetrazzini"
  "Pheasant with Orange Stuffing"

Turner, Elsie, *Fifty Ways of Cooking a Pheasant*. London: Spottiswoode, Ballantyne & Co., rev. 1936, unpaged.
  "Derbyshire Method of Cooking Pheasant"
  "Indian Method of Cooking Pheasant"
  "Italian Method of Cooking Pheasant"
  "Lincolnshire Method of Cooking Pheasant"
  "Norwegian Method of Cooking Pheasant"
  "Croquettes of Pheasant"
  "Galantine of Pheasant"
  "Jellied Pheasant"
  "Kromeskies of Pheasant"
  "Mousse of Pheasant"
  "Timbale of Pheasant"
  "Pheasant in Half Mourning"
  . . . and other pheasant recipes . . .

PORCUPINE and HEDGEHOG

Boorman, Sylvia, *Wild plums in brandy: A cookery book of wild foods in Canada*. Toronto: McGraw-Hill Co. of Canada, 1962, 176 pp.
  "Roast Porcupine"

Kenyon, John, *Mangoes and Monsoons: The Best of Tropical Cooking*. London: Andre Deutsch, 1964, 192 pp.
  "Porcupine in Okra Soup"

Rywell, Martin, *Wild Game Cook Book*. Harriman, Tenn.: Pioneer Press, 1952, 1966, 72 pp.
  (directions for cleaning)
  "Boiled Porcupine"
  "Sauteed Porcupine"

Searle, Townley, *Strange News from China: a first Chinese cookery book*. New York: E. P. Dutton & Co., 1933, 231 pp.
  "Hedgehog Broiled with Lotus in a Ball"

PRONGHORN

FitzGibbon, Theodora, *Game Cooking: A Collection of Recipes with a Dictionary of Rare Game*. London: Andre Deutsch, 1963, 254 pp.
  "Biltong"
  "Braised Antelope"
  "Roast Leg of Antelope, with Mint Sauce"

Herter, George Leonard and Jacques P., *Professional Guide's Manual*. Waseca, Minn.: Herter's, 1960, 349 pp.
  "How to Make Jerky"
  "Pemican"

Karry, Ted, *The Sportsman's Cookbook: for the Hunter and the Fisherman*. Garden City, N.Y.: Doubleday & Co., 1961, 214 pp.
  "Antelope Kabobs"
  "Roast Leg of Antelope"

Melville, Betty, *The Hunter's Cookbook*. Austin, Tex.: Little House Press, 1972, 141 pp.
  (13 antelope recipes)

QUAIL

Atherton, Maxine, *Every Sportsman's Cookbook*. London and New York: The Macmillan Co., 1962, 335 pp.
  "Quail and Veal on Toast"
  "Quail Roasted in Coals"
  "Quail with Ham"

Barnett, Harriet and James, *Game and Fish Cookbook: Including Recipes from* Game Cookery *by Raymond Camp*. New York: Grossman Publishers, 1968, 162 pp.
  "Broiled Quail Roberts"
  "Quail Gallo"
  "Quail in Aspic"
  "Partridge Casserole with Lentils"

RABBIT

Johnson, L. W. "Bill" "The Hunter", *Wild Game Cookbook*. New York: The Benjamin Co., 1968, 160 pp.
  (directions for cleaning)
  "Baked Rabbit Milanese"
  "Batter-Fried Rabbit"
  "English Rabbit Pie"
  "Georgia Rabbit Stew"
  "Hare or Rabbit Salmi"
  "Hasenpfeffer" (3 varieties)
  "Molded Rabbit"
  "Rabbit Creole"
  "Rabbit Park Avenue"
  "Rabbit Salad"
  "Rabbit with Fruit Gravy"
  "Roast Rabbit with Potato Stuffing"
  "Snowshoe Rabbit Bake"
  . . . and other rabbit and hare recipes . . .

Simon, André L., *Guide to Good Food and Wines: A Concise Encyclopaedia of Gastronomy*. London: Collins Press, 1956, 816 pp.
  (discussion of types of rabbits and hares)
  "Galantine of Rabbit (Glendelvine)"
  "Hare (Flanders Style)"
  "Hare Omelette"
  "Hare Soup (Scots style) Bawd Bree"
  "Jugged Hare"
  "Lapin Chasseur"
  "Le Civet de Lapin"
  "Roman Pie (Rabbit)"
  "Stuffed Roast Rabbit"
  . . . and other rabbit and hare recipes . . .

RACCOON

Graham, Gladys R., *Tropical Cooking: A Handbook of Tropical Foods and How to Use Them*. Panama, Repub. of Pan.: The Panama American Press, 1947, 130 pp.
  "Roast Raccoon"
  "Raccoon and Sweet Potatoes"
  "Roast Coati"

Johnson, L. W. "Bill" "The Hunter," *Wild Game Cookbook*. New York: The Benjamin Co., 1968, 160 pp.
  (directions for cleaning)
  "Camp-Roast Raccoon"
  "Corn-Fried Raccoon"
  "Curried Raccoon"
  "Illinois Raccoon Supper"
  "Kraut-Roasted Raccoon"
  "Marinated Raccoon, Hot Beer Style"
  "Molded Raccoon Salad"
  "Raccoon Feed for a Crowd"
  "Raccoon Pie"
  "Raccoon in Sour Cream Sauce"
  "Sage-Stuffed Raccoon"
  "Sweet-Sour Raccoon"
  . . . and other raccoon recipes . . .

Nagel, Werner O., *Cy Littlebee's Guide to Fish & Game*. Jefferson City, Mo.: Missouri Conservation Comm., 1960, 131 pp.
  "Baked Coon (Miz. John Kroeck)"
  "Chicken-Fried Coon (Miz. Frank Roney)"
  "Hunter's Salad—Raccoon (Ray Parker)"
  "Roast Coon, Livingston Style (Miz. Henry S. Ewing)"
  "Roasted Coon (Miz. Clarence Church)"

RATTLESNAKE

COLEMAN, ARTHUR and BOBBIE, *The Texas Cookbook*. New York: A. A. Wyn, 1949, 256 pp.
  "Fried Rattlesnake Meat"
  "Valley Rattlesnake Stew"

EASTLAKE, MARTHA, *Rattlesnake Under Glass*. New York: Simon and Schuster, 1965, 215 pp.
  "Broiled Rattlesnake"
  "Fried Rattlesnake"
  "Pop's Rattlesnake Recipe"

EXPLORERS CLUB, *The Explorers Cookbook*. Caldwell, Idaho: The Caxton Printers, 1971, 235 pp.
  "Boa Constrictor Salad"
  "Braised Boa"
  "Diamondback Rattlesnake Cutlets à la Nyarit"
  "Pepper Python"

REINDEER

CLEVELAND, BESS A., *Alaskan Cookbook*. Berkeley, Calif.: Howell-North, 1960, 164 pp.
  "Brooks Range Canned Caribou"
  "Standing Rib Roast of Caribou"
  "Swiss Steak Caribou"
  "Barrow Reindeer Roast"
  "Nome Reindeer—Rice Curry"
  "Roast Saddle of Reindeer"

UNIVERSITY OF ALASKA COOPERATIVE EXTENSION SERVICE, *Reindeer Recipes*. College, Alaska: University of Alaska and U.S. Dept. of Agriculture, publ. no. 35, undated, 10 pp.
  "Baked Stuffed Reindeer Heart"
  "Favorite Reindeer Meat Loaf"
  "Reindeer Stuffed Cabbage Rolls"
  "Reindeer Stroganoff"
  . . . and other reindeer recipes . . .

SALMON

BOAS, FRANZ, "Ethnology of the Kwakiutl." Washington, D.C.: U.S. Bureau of American Ethnology, 35th Annual Report (1921): 305–601.
  "Blistered Salmon"
  "Preserved Salmon-Heads"
  "Salmon Cheeks"
  "Salmon Fins and Tails"
  "Salmon-Spawn with Salmon-Berry Sprouts"
  "Scorched Salmon"
  "Soaked Green Salmon"
  . . . and 27 other salmon recipes . . .

FIELD, MICHAEL, *Michael Field's Culinary Classics and Improvisations*. New York: Alfred A. Knopf, 1967, 223 pp.
  "A Classic Whole Salmon Simmered"
  "Cold Salmon Mousse"
  "Coulibiac" (Russian)
  "Gratin of Crêpes Stuffed with Salmon and Mushrooms"
  "Salmon Spinach Soufflé"
  "Salmon-Stuffed Eggs in the French Style"
  . . . and other salmon recipes . . .

FISH AND WILDLIFE SERVICE, *Home Preservation of Fishery Products*, fishery leaflet 18, April 1945, 22 pp. *Spiced and Pickled Seafoods*, fishery leaflet 554, October 1963, 18 pp. Washington, D.C.: U.S. Dept. of the Interior.

FREDRIKSON, KARIN, ed., *The Great Scandinavian Cookbook*, translated from the Swedish and edited by J. AUDREY ELLISON. New York: Crown Publishers, 1966, 734 pp.
  "Salmon Canapés"
  "Salmon in Aspic"
  "Salmon Marinaded, Crisply Fried"
  "Salmon Trout à la Meunière"
  . . . and other salmon recipes . . .

SCALLOP

COX, IAN, ed., *The Scallop: Studies of a shell and its influences on humankind, by eight authors*. PAUL GAULTIER, "The Scallop at the Table," 10 pp. London: Shell Transport and Trading Co., 1957.
  "Scallops à la Nantaise"
  "Scallops à la Newburg"

FISH AND WILDLIFE SERVICE, *How to Cook Scallops*, test kitchen series no. 13. Washington, D.C.: U.S. Dept. of the Interior, 1959, 17 pp.
  "Scallop Amandine"
  "Scallop Croquettes"
  "Scallop Kabobs"
  "Scallop Stuffed Acorn Squash"
  "Scallop Thermidor"
  "Sea Scallop Souffle Snacks"
  "Sweet Sour Barbecued Scallops"
  . . . and other scallop recipes . . .

GIBBONS, EUELL, *Stalking the Blue-Eyed Scallop*. New York: David McKay Co., 1964, 332 pp.
  (information on hunting and cleaning)
  "Scalloped Scallops"
  . . . and other scallop recipes . . .

GREENBERG, EMANUEL and MADELINE, *Whiskey in the Kitchen: The Lively Art of Cooking with Bourbon, Scotch, Rum, Brandy, Gin, Liquers . . . and Kindred Spirits*. New York: The Bobbs-Merrill Co., 1968, 315 pp.
  "Ceviche à la Gibson"
  "Ceviche Mary"
  "Coquille St. Jacques"
  "Daiquiri Ceviche"

SEAL

ALASKA SPORTSMAN MAGAZINE, *The Alaskan Camp Book*. Juneau, Alaska: Alaskan Northwest Publishing Co., 1962, 88 pp.
  "Seal Liver Loaf—Teen Cox"

BARR, BERYL, and BARBARA TURNER SACHS, *The Artists' & Writers' Cookbook*. Sausalito, Calif.: Angel Island Publications, 1961, 288 pp.
  "Seal, Deserters' Island Style—Sidney Peterson"

SHARK

CHENG, F. T., former Chinese Ambassador to the Court of St. James's, *Musings of a Chinese Gourmet*. London: Hutchinson & Co., 1954, 156 pp.
  (information on preparation of fins of varying qualities)

Alexandre Dumas' Dictionary of Cuisine, edited, abridged and translated by LOUIS COLMAN from *La Grand Dictionnaire de Cuisine* (Paris, 1873). New York: Simon and Schuster, 1958, 282 pp.
  "Young Shark Stomachs, with Sauce Supreme"

MILLER, GLORIA BLEY, *The Thousand Recipe Chinese Cookbook*. New York: Atheneum, 1966, 927 pp.
  (information on storing and soaking dried shark's fin)
  "Shark's Fin in Ham Sauce"
  "Shark's Fin Omelet, I and II"
  "Shark's Fin Soup, I and II"

SHEEP

SAHER, LILLA VAN, *Exotic Cookery*. New York: The World Publishing Co., 1964, 172 pp.
  "Baked Lamb, from Lebanon"
  "Lamb Curry, from India"
  "Lamb Sate Kambing, from Indonesia"
  "Royal Pilaf, favorite of Shah Pahlevi of Iran"

SHERRY, KATE, *Specialty Cuts: and how to cook them.* Rutland, Vt. and Tokyo: Charles E. Tuttle Co., 1968, 113 pp.

(200 ways to prepare organ meats)

WILLARD, JOHN, *Game Is Good Eating.* Helena, Mont.: State Publishing Co., 1954, 88 pp.

(information on aging, cleaning and dressing, cooling and hanging, cutting and packaging, freezing big game)
"Bighorn Rib Barbecue"
"Cubed Bighorn Rarebit"
"Mountain Sheep Kebob"

SHRIMP

ALBERSON, SARAH D., *The Blue Sea Cookbook.* New York: Hastings House, 1968, 290 pp.
"Gourmet Flamed Scampi"
"Hot Shrimp with Red Devil Sauce"
"Shrimp Aloha"
"Shrimp-Stuffed Eggplant"
"Shrimp Tipsy"
. . . and other shrimp recipes . . .

ROBOTTI, FRANCES D. and PETER J., *French Cooking in the New World.* Garden City, N.Y.: Doubleday & Co., 1967, 510 pp.
"Cajun Curried Shrimp"
"Creole Shrimp"
"East Indian Shrimp Sauce"
"New Orleans Dixie-fried Shrimp"
"Shrimp Remoulade"
. . . and other shrimp recipes . . .

SCHULZ, EVA JEAN, *Shrimply Delicious!* Garden City, N.Y.: Doubleday & Co., 354 pp.
. . . over 600 shrimp recipes . . .

SNAIL

GERBER, HILDA, *Traditional Cookery of the Cape Malays: Food Customs and 200 Old Cape Recipes.* Cape Town, U.S.A.: A. A. Balkema, 1957, 127 pp.
"Periwinkles (Perdevoetjies)"
"Curried Periwinkles (Perdevoetjies in Kerrie)"

GIBBONS, EUELL, *Stalking the Blue-Eyed Scallop.* New York: David Mckay Co., 1964, 332 pp.
(information on gathering and cleaning)
"Boiled Periwinkles"
"Periwinkle Fritters"
"Periwinkle Omelet"

MONTAGNÉ, PROSPER, *Larousse Gastronomique: The Encyclopedia of Food, Wine & Cookery.* Paris: Augé, Gillon, Hollier-Larousse, Moreau et Cie (Librairie Larousse), 1938. New York: Crown Publishers, 1961, 1101 pp.
"Snails à l'arlésienne"
"Snails à la bourguignonne"
"Snail broth"
"Snails à la chablaisienne"
"Snails Comtesse Riguidi"
"Snails à la poulette"

SQUIRREL

American Heritage Cookbook: and Illustrated History of American Eating & Drinking. New York: American Heritage Publishing Co., 1964, 383 pp.
"Brunswick Stew"
"Burgoo"

CAMP, RAYMOND R., *Game Cookery in America and Europe.* New York: Coward-McCann, 1958, 252 pp.
"Fried Squirrel Arkansas"
"Squirrel Casserole Fours"
"Squirrel Marsala"
"Squirrel Pie"
"Squirrel Stew Albury"
"Wild Acres Squirrel"

TURKEY

BEARD, JAMES, *Fowl and Game Cookery.* New York: M. Barrows & Co., 1944, 196 pp.
"Boiled Turkey in Parchment"
"North American Wild Turkey"
"Roasting Method I, II"
"Smoked Turkey"
"Special Turkey Soup"
"Turkey in Aspic"
. . . and other turkey recipes . . .

NATIONAL TURKEY FEDERATION, *Turkey Handbook.* Mount Morris, Ill., 1960, 73 pp.
Turkey recipes for main dishes, salads, sandwiches, soups & stews, loaves & hash, stuffings, gravies & sauces, pies & cakes, giblets. Methods for roasting, steaming, broiling, frying, barbecueing, carving.

RANHOFER, CHARLES, *The Epicurean: a complete treatise of analytical and practical studies on the culinary art, by the former chef of Delmonico's.* Chicago: The Hotel Monthly Press, 1920, 1183 pp.
"Small Turkey à la Financière"
"Turkey—Grenades—à la Jules Verne"
"Turkey Truffled and Garnished with Black Olives"
. . . and other turkey recipes . . .

TURTLE

Gourmet Cookbook, The. New York: Gourmet Distributing Corp., Vol. I, 1950, 781 pp.
(information on cleaning)
"Broiled Turtle Steak"
"Snapper Turtle Soup"
"Terrapin Stew Baltimore"
"Terrapin Stew Philadelphia"
"Turtle Steaks Marchand de Vin"
"Turtle Steak Sauté"
Vol. II, 1957, 753 pp.
"Turtle Pie"
"Turtle Steaks in White Wine"

MILORADOVICH, MILO, *The Art of Fish Cookery.* Garden City, N.Y.: Garden City Books, 1949, 457 pp.
(directions for cleaning)
"Green Turtle Broth with Sherry"
"Terrapin Creamed American Style"
"Terrapin Madeira"
"Turtle Bourgeoise"
"Turtle Steak Rosemary"

WATTS, EDITH BALLARD, *Jesse's Book of Creole and Deep South Recipes.* New York: The Viking Press, 1954, 184 pp.
"Ragout of Diamond-Back Terrapin"

WHALE

MILORADOVICH, MILO, *The Art of Fish Cookery.* Garden City, N.Y.: Garden City Books, 1949, 457 pp.
"Whalemeat Fillet with Mushrooms"
"Whale Pot Roast Seattle"

SCHULTZ, SIGRID, ed., *Overseas Press Club Cookbook.* Garden City, N.Y.: Doubleday & Co., 1962, 370 pp.
"Muktuk"

TRYCKARE, TRE, *The Whale.* New York: Simon and Schuster, 1968, 287 pp.
(information on whale meat)

ZEBRA

GUGGISBERG, ROSANNE, *Eating in Africa.* Cape Town, U.S.A.: Howard Timmins, 1958, 247 pp.
"Zebra Stew"

GUY, CHRISTIAN, *An Illustrated History of French Cuisine: from Charlemagne to Charles de Gaulle,* translated by ELISABETH ABBOTT. New York: Bramhall House, 1962, 243 pp.
(discussion of donkey and horse meat)

Tin-enameled earthenware tureen
molded in the form of a tub full of *fish.*
The head of the central fish
is raised to form a handle on the cover.
From Rato, Portugal, Brunetto period, about 1770.
Height 11 5/8 inches.
Courtesy of Campbell Museum, Camden, #1968019.

MEAT AND SEAFOOD SOURCES

LISTED BELOW *are a few suppliers from whom the more unusual fresh or frozen meats may be purchased. Stocks vary, depending on season, demand, and law. Commercially-sold meats of "wild" animals often come from licensed game farms. Whatever the source, rigid laws are enforced as to rearing, butchering, selling, and shipping these meats. Items listed in parentheses do not necessarily comprise the complete stock of the seller, and products may or may not be available on a regular basis. Sellers whose names are preceded by a star (*) accept mail orders from individuals and ship fresh/frozen meats by air, railway express, or bus. Names qualified as "wholesale only" or "distributor only" should be contacted through a local retailer.*

ALABAMA

Possum Growers and Breeders Association of America, Inc.
c/o Frank ("Eat More Possum") B. Clark
Big C Possum Ranch
Clanton, Alabama
Phone: (205) 755–0182
(opossum)

ARIZONA

Carl's Eastern Meats and Sea Foods
7150 East Thomas Road
Scottsdale, Arizona 85251
Phone: (602) 947–9783
(abalone, octopus, mussels, frogs' legs, pheasant, quail)

ARKANSAS

Pel-Freez Rabbit Meat, Inc.
Post Office Box 68
Rogers, Arkansas 72756
Phone: (501) 636–4361
(domestic farm-raised rabbit, USDA inspected Grade A, sold through major meat distributors and national food chains)

CALIFORNIA

* Kwong On Lung Importers
686 North Spring Street
Los Angeles, California 90012
Phone: (213) 628–1069
(dried shark's fin)

Draeger's
1010 University Drive
Menlo Park, California 94025
Phone: (415) 322–2339
(goat, rabbit, squab, quail, pheasant, guinea fowl, abalone, mussels, octopus, squid, frogs' legs)

Piedmont Grocery
4038 Piedmont Avenue
Oakland, California 94611
Phone: (415) 653–8181
(rabbit, squab, quail, pheasant, guinea fowl, abalone, mussels, octopus, frogs' legs)

Jurgensen's Grocery Company
842 East California Boulevard
Pasadena, California 91106
Phone: (213) 792–3121
also
409 North Beverly Drive
Beverly Hills, California 90210
Phone: (213) 274–8611
(venison, quail, special orders)

Petrini's
2055 McAllister Street
San Francisco, California 94118
Phone: (415) 567–3909
also
270 Bon Air Shopping Center
Greenbrae, California 94904
Phone: (415) 461–1590
(goat, rabbit, squab, quail, pheasant, guinea fowl, abalone, mussels, octopus, squid, eel, frogs' legs)

* Durham Meat Company
160 Sunol Street
Post Office Box 4230
San Jose, California 95126
Phone: (408) 298–6404
(buffalo from Wyoming ranch)

* Goat City
18999 West Highway 140
Stevinson, California 95374
Phone: (209) 634–5932
(wild lamb and goats for barbecue)

DISTRICT OF COLUMBIA

Cannon Seafood, Inc.
1065 31st Street Northwest
Washington, D.C. 20015
Phone: retail (202) 337–8366
        wholesale (202) 337–3710
(mussels, snails, octopus, eel, turtle)

The Denali Directory to game species, seasons, and guides, in the *NRA Hunting Annual*, is sold at sporting goods stores and at book stores and has editorial offices at 1600 Rhode Island Avenue, NW, Washington, D.C. 20036.

International Safeway
1110 F Street Northwest
Washington, D.C. 20004
Phone: (202) 628–1880
(buffalo, venison, cottontail rabbit, Muscovy duck, wild turkey, pheasant, squab)

ILLINOIS

J. Manaster Company
1235 West George Street
Chicago, Illinois 60657
Phone: (312) 248-9000
(wholesaler: venison, African lion, wild boar, hippopotamus, elk, moose, raccoon, rabbit (Australian wild, Polish, Chinese), pheasant, quail, Mallard duck, guinea fowl, squab, rattlesnake)

* Czimer Foods, Inc.
159th Street between Parker and Bell
  Roads on Route 7
Lockport, Illinois 60441
Phone: (815) 838-3503
(peacock, wild turkey, Canada goose, Mallard duck, guinea fowl, pheasant, hippopotamus, lion, mountain sheep, caribou, wild goat, wild boar, beaver, opossum, raccoon, moose, reindeer, elk, antelope, bear, buffalo)

North American Game Breeders and Shooting Preserves Association has 3,200 licensed preserves in its membership. Information on a particular geographical area or type of preserve may be obtained by writing the association's secretary, Dr. Edward L. Kozicky, Olin Winchester-Western East Alton, Illinois 62024.

MICHIGAN

Schaefer Road Seafood Fish &
  Poultry Market
5703 Schaefer Road
Dearborn, Michigan 48126
Phone: (313) LU1-0220
(octopus, squid, eel, frogs' legs, mussels)

MINNESOTA

Crown Meat and Provision Co., Inc.
443 Hoover Street Northeast
Minneapolis, Minnesota 55413
Phone: (612) 331-4660
(wholesale: venison, elk)

MISSOURI

Mateker's Gourmet Meat Shop, Inc.
11808 Tesson Ferry Road
St. Louis, Missouri 63128
Phone: (314) 842-4100
(rabbit, quail, squab, frogs' legs, mussels, snails)

Reese Finer Foods
400 South Fourth Street
St. Louis, Missouri 63166
Phone: (314) 621-5400
(processor and distributor of diverse and unusual canned meats)

NEBRASKA

* Prairie Pride Farms
Box 517
Grand Island, Nebraska 68801
Phone: (308) 384-8590
(quail, pheasant)

NEW YORK

* Zeldner's Wild Game Center
638 Clinton Street
Buffalo, New York 14210
Phone: (716) 853-3737
(hippopotamus, African lion, water buffalo, elephant, kangaroo, bear, reindeer, moose, elk, antelope, wild boar, chamois, raccoon, opossum, beaver, nine varieties of rabbit. Seal flippers, shark steaks, freshwater turtles, eel. Mallard duck, Canada goose, wild turkey, pheasant, quail. Seventeen smoked specialties.)

Jefferson Market
455 Sixth Avenue
New York, New York 10011
Phone: (212) OR5-2277
(venison, rabbit, pheasant, guinea fowl, frogs' legs, octopus, mussels, snails)

M. Lobel & Sons Inc.
1096 Madison Avenue
  (82nd/83rd Streets)
New York, New York 10028
Phone: (212) RE7-1372
(wild suckling pig, venison, buffalo, bear, goat, wild turkey, wild duck, pheasant, quail, squab, guinea fowl)

* Maryland Midtown Gourmet
1072 First Avenue
New York, New York 10022
Phone: (212) 595-1500
(most of the unusual meats in this cookbook were obtained from this market)

Ottomanelli's Meat Market
281 Bleecker Street
New York, New York 10014
Phone: (212) OR5-4217
(venison, wild boar, goat, rabbit, quail, pheasant, guinea fowl, wild turkey, wild duck, partridge)

PENNSYLVANIA

Dick's Delicacies
Reading Terminal Market
Philadelphia, Pennsylvania 19107
Phone: (215) WA2-6669
(wild Australian hare, Australian rabbit, venison, pheasant, quail)

SOUTH DAKOTA

* Director, Custer State Park
Hermosa, South Dakota 57744
(605) 255-4515
(buffalo)

TEXAS

Glatzmaier Seafood Market
416 Travis Street
Houston, Texas 77002
Phone: (713) 223-3331
(octopus, squid, abalone, turtle, clams, frogs' legs)

Jim Jamail & Sons Food Market
3114 Kirby Drive
Houston, Texas 77006
Phone: (713) 523-5535
(cabrito, quail, squab, rabbit, red salmon, scallops, squid)

WYOMING

* Bison Pete
Post Office Box 96
Wheatland, Wyoming 82201
Phone: (307) 322-9680
(buffalo)

CANADA

Brendean Game Farm & Hunting
  Preserve
Rural Route 4
Uxbridge, Ontario
Phone: (416) 985-3382 (Port Perry)
(pheasant, partridge)

The Lobster Cove
516 Eglinton West
Toronto, Ontario
Phone: (416) 483-1755
(eel, octopus, squid, frogs' legs, mussels)

Twenty Valley Game Farm &
  Hunting Preserve
Rural Route 1
Jordan Station, Ontario
Phone: (416) 562-4281
(pheasant, partridge)

Boucherie Raymond
4025 Jean Talon East
Montreal, Quebec
Phone: (514) 722-9621
(horse)

Canadian Meat Company
1195 St. Lawrence
Montreal, Quebec
Phone: (514) 861-9997
(venison, moose, rabbit, pheasant, quail)

ENGLAND

Randall & Aubin, Ltd., Charcuterie
16 Brewer Street (Soho)
London W1, England
Phone: 01-4373507
(venison, frogs' legs, snails)

Richards Ltd., Fishmonger
11 Brewer Street (Soho)
London W1, England
Phone: 01-4371358
(octopus, cuttlefish)

FRANCE

Delaunay-Leveillé
13, Rue Marbeuf
Paris 8
Phone: 225.25.51
(fowl and game)

Sevenet
57, Rue de Passy
Paris 16
Phone: 228.21.73
(fish, fowl)

WILDLIFE CONSERVATION DEPARTMENTS

Each state in the United States currently licenses an average of 500 game farms—some private, some commercial. (Wisconsin, for example, licenses about 1,300; Iowa, about 500.) Information on these farms may be obtained by writing state wildlife conservation departments:

Department of Conservation and Natural Resources
Game and Fish Division
64 North Union Street
Montgomery, Alabama 36104
Phone: (205) 269–6701

Alaska Department of Fish and Game
Subport Building
Juneau, Alaska 99801
Phone: (907) 586–3392

Arizona Game and Fish Department
2222 West Greenway Road
Phoenix, Arizona 85023
Phone: (602) 942–3000

Arkansas Game and Fish Commission
2 Capitol Mall
Little Rock, Arkansas 72201
Phone: (501) 371–1025

California Fish and Game Commission
1416 Ninth Street
Sacramento, California 95814
Phone: (916) 445–5656

Colorado Division of Wildlife
6060 North Broadway
Denver, Colorado 80216
Phone: (303) 825–1192

Connecticut Department of Environmental Protection
State Office Building
165 Capitol Avenue
Hartford, Connecticut 06115
Phone: (203) 566–3356

Department of Natural Resources and Environmental Control
Division of Fish and Wildlife
D Street
Dover, Delaware 19901
Phone: (302) 678–4431

Florida Game and Fresh Water Fish Commission
620 South Meridian
Tallahassee, Florida 32304
Phone: (904) 224–0115

Georgia Department of Natural Resources
Trinity-Washington Building
270 Washington Street Southwest
Atlanta, Georgia 30334
Phone: (404) 656–3500

Hawaii Division of Fish and Game
1179 Punchbowl Street
Honolulu, Hawaii 96813
Phone: (808) 548–5917

Idaho Fish and Game Department
600 South Walnut
P.O. Box 25
Boise, Idaho 83707
Phone: (208) 384–3700

Illinois Department of Conservation
605 State Office Building
Springfield, Illinois 62706
Phone: (271) 525–6302

Indiana Division of Fish and Wildlife
607 State Office Building
Indianapolis, Indiana 46204
Phone: (317) 633–5658

Iowa Conservation Commission
300 Fourth Street
Des Moines, Iowa 50319
Phone: (515) 281–5971

Kansas Forestry, Fish and Game Commission
P.O. Box 1028
Pratt, Kansas 67124
Phone: (316) 672–6473

Kentucky Department of Fish and Wildlife Resources
Capital Plaza
Frankfort, Kentucky 40601
Phone: (502) 564–3400

Louisiana Wildlife and Fisheries Commission
400 Royal Street
New Orleans, Louisiana 70130
Phone: (504) 527–5126

Maine Department of Inland Fisheries and Game
State Office Building
Augusta, Maine 04330
Phone: (207) 289–3371

Maryland Department of Natural Resources
Rowe Boulevard and Taylor Avenue
Annapolis, Maryland 21401
Phone: (301) 267–5186

Massachusetts Division of Fisheries and Game
State Office Building
100 Cambridge Street
Boston, Massachusetts 02202
Phone: (617) 727–3151

Michigan Department of Natural Resources
Mason Building
Lansing, Michigan 48926
Phone: (517) 373–1230

Minnesota Division of Game and Fish
390 Centennial Building
658 Cedar Street
St. Paul, Minnesota 55155
Phone: (612) 296–2894

Mississippi Game and Fish Commission
P.O. Box 451
Jackson, Mississippi 39205
Phone: (601) 354–7333

Missouri Department of Conservation
North Ten Mile Drive
Jefferson City, Missouri 65101
Phone: (314) 751–4115

Montana Department of Fish and Game
Helena, Montana 59601
Phone: (406) 449–2535

Nebraska Game and Parks Commission
P.O. Box 30370
Lincoln, Nebraska 68503
Phone: (402) 434–0641

Nevada Department of Fish and Game
P.O. Box 10678
Reno, Nevada 89510
Phone: (702) 784–6214

New Hampshire Fish and Game Department
34 Bridge Street
Concord, New Hampshire 03301
Phone: (603) 271–3421

New Jersey Division of Fish, Game and Shellfisheries
P.O. Box 1809
Trenton, New Jersey 08625
Phone: (609) 292–2965

New Mexico Department of Game and Fish
State Capitol
Santa Fe, New Mexico 87801
Phone: (505) 827–2651

New York Department of Environmental Conservation
Division of Fish and Wildlife
50 Wolf Road
Albany, New York 12201
Phone: (518) 457–5690

North Carolina Wildlife Resources Commission
Albemarle Building
325 North Salisbury Street
Raleigh, North Carolina 27611
Phone: (919) 829–3391

North Dakota State Game and Fish Department
2121 Lovett Avenue
Bismark, North Dakota 58501
Phone: (701) 224–2180

Ohio Division of Wildlife
Department of Natural Resources
1500 Dublin Road
Columbus, Ohio 43212
Phone: (614) 469–4603

Oklahoma Department of Wildlife Conservation
1801 North Lincoln
P.O. Box 53465
Oklahoma City, Oklahoma 73105
Phone: (405) 521–3851

Oregon State Game Commission
1634 Southwest Alder Street
P.O. Box 3503
Portland, Oregon 97208
Phone: (503) 229–5551

Pennsylvania Game Commission
P.O. Box 1567
Harrisburg, Pennsylvania 17120
Phone: (717) 787–3633

Rhode Island Department of Natural Resources
Veterans' Memorial Building
Providence, Rhode Island 02903
Phone: (401) 277–2285

South Carolina Wildlife and Marine Resources Department
1015 Main Street
P.O. Box 167
Columbia, South Carolina 29202
Phone: (803) 758–2561

South Dakota Department of Game, Fish and Parks
State Office Building
Pierre, South Dakota 57501
Phone: (605) 224–3485

Tennessee Game and Fish Commission
P.O. Box 40747, Ellington Agricultural Center
Nashville, Tennessee 37220
Phone: (615) 741–1421

Texas Parks and Wildlife Commission
John H. Reagan Building
Austin, Texas 78701
Phone: (512) 475–2087

Utah Division of Wildlife Resources
1596 West North Temple
Salt Lake City, Utah 84116
Phone: (801) 328–5081

Vermont Fish and Game Department
Montpelier, Vermont 05602
Phone: (802) 828–3371

Virginia Commission of Game and Inland Fisheries
P.O. Box 11104
Richmond, Virginia 23230
Phone: (703) 770–4974

Washington Game Department
600 North Capital Way
Olympia, Washington 98501
Phone: (206) 753–5700

West Virginia Department of Natural Resources
1800 Washington Street
East Charleston, West Virginia 25305
Phone: (304) 348–2754

Wisconsin Department of Natural Resources
Division of Fish and Game
P.O. Box 450
Madison, Wisconsin 43701
Phone: (608) 266–1877

Wyoming Game and Fish Commission
P.O. Box 1589
Cheyenne, Wyoming 82001
Phone: (307) 777–7461

Department of Lands and Forests
109th Street and 99th Avenue
Edmonton 6, Alberta, Canada
Phone: (403) 229–4461

British Columbia Fish and Wildlife Branch
Department of Recreation and Conservation
Parliament Buildings
Victoria, British Columbia, Canada
Phone: (604) 382–6111

Recreation and Cultural Affairs
408 Norquay Building
Winnipeg, Manitoba, Canada
Phone: (204) 946–7533

New Brunswick Department of Natural Resources
Fish and Wildlife Branch
Centennial Building
Fredericton, New Brunswick, Canada

Newfoundland Wildlife Department
Confederation Building
St. John's, Newfoundland, Canada
Phone: (709) 722–0711

Superintendent of Game
Government of the Northwest Territories
Yellowknife, Northwest Territories, Canada

Fish and Wildlife Division
Environmental Control Commission
Charlottetown, Prince Edward Island, Canada

Nova Scotia Division of Wildlife Conservation
P.O. Box 516
Kentville, Nova Scotia, Canada
Phone: (902) 678–4198

Ministry of Natural Resources
Parliament Buildings
Toronto, Ontario, Canada
Phone: (416) 365–4251

Quebec Department of Tourism, Fish and Game
Parliament Buildings
Quebec City, Quebec, Canada
Phone: (418) 693–2220

Saskatchewan Wildlife Branch
Department of Natural Resources
Government Administration Building
Regina, Saskatchewan, Canada
Phone: (306) 522–1691

Yukon Territory Game Department
Box 2703
Whitehorse, Yukon Territory, Canada
Phone: (403) 667–5228

Northwest Coastal Indian feast dish
carved in wood to represent a *sea otter*.
From Vancouver Island.
Courtesy of Field Museum of Natural History,
Chicago, #19116.

166

Kwakiutl feast dish
carved in wood to represent a *seal*.
Used mainly to serve fish oil
which was ladled into smaller dishes.
Courtesy of Field Museum of Natural History,
Chicago, #85079.

INDEX

INDEX TO NATURAL HISTORIES

(Numbers in *italics* refer to illustrations)

Bronze container for spices, in the form of a *frog.*
Flemish or German, fifteenth century.
Courtesy of The Duke University Museum of Art, Durham, #1966.28.

INDEX TO RECIPES AND FOODS

(Recipes are shown in CAPITAL LETTERS)

Porcelain platter with painting of *rhinoceros*, after woodcut by Albrecht Dürer, adapted at Chelsea, England, 1752–6. Length 12¾ inches, width 9¾ inches. The Metropolitan Museum of Art, New York; collection of Irwin Untermyer.

INDEX TO ILLUSTRATIONS: ARTISTS, CULTURES, PROVENIENCES, MEDIUMS